Research and Writing in International Relations

Second Edition

SHARON **SPRAY**

Elon University

LAURA **ROSELLE**

Elon University

Longman

Boston Columbus Indianapolis New York San Francisco Upper Saddle River
Amsterdam Cape Town Dubai London Madrid Milan Munich Paris Montreal Toronto
Delhi Mexico City São Paulo Sydney Hong Kong Seoul Singapore Taipei Tokyo

Senior Acquisitions Editor: Vikram Mukhija
Editorial Assistant: Beverly Fong
Senior Marketing Manager: Lindsey Prudhomme
Production Project Manager: Clara Bartunek
Project Coordination, Text Design, and Electronic Page Makeup: Saraswathi
    Muralidhar/PreMediaGlobal
Creative Art Director: Jayne Conte
Cover Designer: Suzanne Duda
Printer and Binder: STP Courier/Westford
Cover Printer: STP Courier/Moore Langen

Library of Congress Cataloging-in-Publication Data
Spray, Sharon L.
  Research and writing in international relations/Sharon Spray, Laura Roselle.—2nd ed.
     p. cm.
  Includes bibliographical references and index.
  ISBN-13: 978-0-205-06065-8
  ISBN-10: 0-205-06065-X
  1. International relations—Research—Handbooks, manuals, etc.   I. Roselle, Laura.   II. Title.
  JZ1234.S77 2012
  327.1072—dc22

                                                                              2010050523

Copyright © 2012, 2008 by Pearson Education, Inc.

Longman
is an imprint of

www.pearsonhighered.com

2 3 4 5 6 7 8 9 10—CRW—14 13

ISBN-13: 978-0-205-06065-8
ISBN-10:   0-205-06065-X

BRIEF CONTENTS

DETAILED CONTENTS

PART III   Writing Resources   123

CHAPTER 10
Organizing Sources and Notes   124

CHAPTER 11
Citing Sources   132

CHAPTER 12
Following Style Guidelines   140

PREFACE

S ince the first edition of *Research and Writing in International Relations,* was published in 2008, the availability of resources for student research has increased substantially. New sources include blog-post databases, intergovernmental organization databases, new academic journal databases, and even create-your-own databases. A simple word search of the term "terrorism" on the academic journal archive, JSTOR, now yields over 17,000 article citations; and, entering the term "migration" yields over 154,000 articles. Students now have access to hundreds of thousands of YouTube videos—many of which document important moments in world affairs. Information access is growing exponentially. What we continually hear from our students is that they have genuine interests in the world around them and for conducting research in international relations but they often do not know how or where to start a research project amid so much information. Figuring out how to narrow the scope of discovery and organize the research and writing process is an ever increasing challenging.

The second edition of *Research and Writing in International Relations* retains all of the elements of our first book that have helped hundreds of students in introductory and upper-level international relations courses simplify the research and writing process. We use a case-based approach in which we provide guidance and examples for how to move beyond a general topic to developing a research question, clear steps that help navigate the literature review process, guidance in how to set up a plan for gathering and organizing evidence, tips for analyzing information and section by section instruction for writing a comprehensive research paper. Most importantly, however, this text still contains the feature that no other international studies text on research and writing in the market contains—a set of chapters devoted specifically to topics that help students develop interesting case-based research topics. In sum, this entire book is designed to help students move efficiently through each step of the research process and complete a quality research project while learning valuable research skills that can be used for many research projects.

NEW TO THIS EDITION

New to this edition are several topical chapters in areas of interest to students today. These chapters contain research question ideas, citations for important literature on these topics; and as did our previous edition, these chapters identify credible resources to get students started with quality projects. This second edition also contains more detailed discussions on how to identify and work with the scholarly literature, how to clarify, define, and organize the research process, and more instruction on how to write a literature review. All updates in this text were completed with the goal of keeping the text's most complimented features: it is concise, easy to use, focused on the organizational aspects of research and writing, provides students with good examples and resources, and most of all—it helps students develop more advanced papers by helping them with step-by-step descriptions, examples, and resources at every step of the paper-writing process. Highlights of this second edition include:

- new chapters on globalization, US foreign policy, international political economy and international organizations and law;
- new ideas for student projects including new starter questions for case-based projects including questions on human rights, international communications, the internet, terrorism and national security;
- updated sources for gathering project data;
- more fully developed instruction for research and writing literature reviews;
- improved instruction for gathering variable evidence including a revised check off sheet and enhanced examples; and
- more detailed instruction for helping students move from evidence gathering to actually writing their final papers.

FEATURES

This book is still designed as a brief supplemental text for international relations courses at all levels. Part I of the text presents the research process in a series of steps appropriate for the completion of a twenty-five page paper in the field of international relations. As in the previous text, Part I is divided so that various parts of paper development can be focused upon independent of one another. The four chapters in Part I are divided as follows. Chapter 1, on question development contains information about how to begin research and choose a general topic, how to develop an initial question, what dependent and independent variables are, and how to refine the question. Chapter 2 covers the literature review in international relations, describing what scholarly sources are, why students should use them, how to find them, and how to organize them. Chapter 3 discusses methodology and covers how students can operationalize and measure variables. Chapter 4 on analysis and writing discusses how students analyze what they find and describes the process of writing. Here we give a breakdown of the research paper, with approximate page lengths for each section.

All chapters in Part I have several features that distinguish this text from other research writing texts in the field. The first is that each chapter in Part I includes textboxes, tables, and figures that provide students with simple-to-understand examples of all of the major concepts we introduce. For example, students often have difficulty narrowing a literature review search. In Chapter 2, we provide an example that starts with a broad topic and then show students how to narrow that topic substantially so that it reduces the amount of literature they must sift through, and helps them narrow their topic of inquiry to one that is amenable to a comparative case-based project. Secondly, to address questions that arise even when all of the examples in the text have been followed, we include "frequently asked questions" sections in these chapters. Our goal of the FAQ sections is to help students learn to do their own problem solving. Therefore, the FAQ sections ask students to reflect on the problems they experience and guide them towards finding answers rather than just providing a "one-size-fits-all" list for them to follow. And finally, because we understand that some concepts take practice to master, we have included assignments and exercises in each chapter in Part I that can be used by instructors to enhance students' research and writing skills. These assignments and exercises are specifically geared towards different phases of the research process and focus on skills we know from teaching our students are helpful in reinforcing simple, but key aspects necessary for mastering project development.

Part II of the book is the section where we provide specific project guidance for students including research questions that can be changed through various case selection methods and identify by topic area *specific* scholarly literature that will assist them in beginning their literature reviews. These chapters also have information associated with relevant databases and information resources that will assist students in project development. As we indicate above, this second edition has several new chapters with each of these chapters introducing new sub-topics and new research project questions. For example, Chapter 5 is on international conflict and national security. Covered in this chapter are student projects associated with levels of violence and projects associated with different types of conflicts. Also included in this chapter are project questions on state interventions and also on terrorism. Like other chapters in this section, Chapter 5 includes over five dozen citations of the most highly influential literature associated with these topics. By providing the citations for influential literature in the field students are able to focus their projects more quickly, learn more efficiently, and master independent research. We have also taken out some of the difficult work of finding data sources for students by providing at least a dozen credible on-line data sources in each chapter that can be used for gathering evidence for their case based projects. The key to this section and this text, however, is that each chapter in Part II provides multiple ways of looking at the topic, with tangible resources to get any student started on a project. Chapter 6 covers U.S. foreign policy suggesting a wide range of projects from looking at foreign policy from the foreign policy angle to more textured state-level analysis. Chapter 7 is on international political economics, and incorporates a number of sub-topics students find particularly interesting including project questions associated with development, gender, world trade, international corruption, and more. International organizations and law are covered in Chapter 8. Included in this chapter is guidance in developing projects on topics such as human rights, war crimes, international environmental issues, and international treaties. The final chapter of this section, Chapter 9, is on globalization and global issues. Here students will find assistance in building projects on topics associated with international media and communications, transnational advocacy, migration, and the internet.

Part III of this text help pull student projects together by covering some of the nuts and bolts of writing, including information on keeping track of resources (Chapter 9), using citations (Chapter 10), and following academic style guidelines (Chapter 11).

While this text focuses on systematic investigation and the case-based approach to research, it was never designed as a methodology text. We use this approach to teach students how to identify questions and variables, to study international relations literature beyond the course textbook, to choose cases and collect information in a systematic and purposeful way, and to draw conclusions based on this careful process. We are not claiming that this is the only way to study international relations, but we have chosen to focus on this method because it promotes a set of skills that are important and valuable for students at all course levels. We have used this text in Introduction to IR courses, upper-level IR courses, and Senior Seminars. We find that this type of research can help students become more critical thinkers, forcing them to explore not only relationships between variables but also the strength of those relationships. Students are taught that they should routinely consider alternative explanations and that not all alternative explanations are of equal weight. Through this process, students are forced to go beyond popular explanations to understand the inherent complexity of political processes and effects. We think this is crucial to the training of students today.

SUPPLEMENTS

Longman is pleased to offer several resources to qualified adopters of *Research and Writing in International Relations* and their students that will make teaching and learning from this book even more effective and enjoyable.

Passport for International Relations

With Passport, choose the resources you want from MyPoliSciKit and put links to them into your course management system. If there is assessment associated with those resources, it also can be uploaded, allowing the results to feed directly into your course management system's gradebook. With over 150 MyPoliSciKit assets like video case studies, mapping exercises, comparative exercises, simulations, podcasts, *Financial Times* newsfeeds, current events quizzes, politics blog, and much more, Passport is available for any Pearson introductory or upper-level political science book. Use ISBN 0-205-0740-81 to order Passport with this book. To learn more, please contact your Pearson representative.

MySearchLab

Need help with a paper? MySearchLab saves time and improves results by offering start-to-finish guidance on the research/writing process and full-text access to academic journals and periodicals. Use ISBN 0-205-07398-0 to order

MySearchLab with this book. To learn more, please visit www.mysearchlab.com or contact your Pearson representative.

The Economist

Every week, *The Economist* analyzes the important happenings around the globe. From business to politics, to the arts and science, its coverage connects seemingly unrelated events in unexpected ways. Use ISBN 0-205-00258-7 to order a 15-week subscription with this book for a small additional charge. To learn more, please contact your Pearson representative.

The Financial Times

Featuring international news and analysis from journalists in more than 50 countries, *The Financial Times* provides insights and perspectives on political and economic developments around the world. Use ISBN 0-205-07393-X to order a 15-week subscription with this book for a small additional charge. To learn more, please contact your Pearson representative.

Longman Atlas of World Issues (0-205-78020-2)

From population and political systems to energy use and women's rights, the *Longman Atlas of World Issues* features full-color thematic maps that examine the forces shaping the world. Featuring maps from the latest edition of *The Penguin State of the World Atlas*, this excerpt includes critical thinking exercises to promote a deeper understanding of how geography affects many global issues. Available at no additional charge when packaged with this book.

Goode's World Atlas (0-321-65200-2)

First published by Rand McNally in 1923, *Goode's World Atlas* has set the standard for college reference atlases. It features hundreds of physical, political, and thematic maps as well as graphs, tables, and a pronouncing index. Available at a discount when packaged with this book.

The Penguin Dictionary of International Relations (0-140-51397-3)

This indispensable reference by Graham Evans and Jeffrey Newnham includes hundreds of cross-referenced entries on the enduring and emerging theories, concepts, and events that are shaping the academic discipline of international relations and today's world politics. Available at a discount when packaged with this book.

ACKNOWLEDGMENTS

We have benefited greatly from and must thank two groups of people: our students and the colleagues who reviewed or contributed suggestions on this manuscript. Our students have challenged us to be clear about our expectations and about why research matters. Our colleagues, including those in our departmental writing group at Elon University—have given us invaluable suggestions, and the manuscript is much stronger due to their careful reading. We would also like to thank the reviewers for the previous edition, whose comments have been invaluable in the revision of this second edition, including Daniel Masters of the University of North Carolina—Wilmington, Jack Moran of Kennesaw State University, and Emmanuel Uwalaka of Webster University. Finally, we would like to thank Vikram Mukhija and Beverly Fong, for their help and guidance throughout this revision. Of course, if you have suggestions and/or comments as you use or consider using this book, we would be more than happy to receive them. Errors or omissions are our own.

The Research
and Writing Process

There is nothing simple about the relationships among states in the international system. States differ in their structures of government, their levels of economic prosperity, their ethnic compositions, and their cultures. No two instances of conflict are ever the same, and cooperation among nations is often tenuous. Levels of international power shift, domestic political structures change, and the wealth of nations fluctuates. Whether it is the democratic election of a new president or a military coup, domestic leadership changes can transform regional and international dynamics in a single day.

International relations cannot be understood merely as the interactions of states or the decisions of world leaders. The power of nonstate actors, such as the World Bank, the United Nations, and nongovernmental organizations (NGOs), influences the actions of nations. Even events unrelated to individual governments—natural disasters, international terrorism, the spread of human disease—can alter international relations. To the casual observer of international politics, it might seem as though one could never make predictions, draw comparisons, or develop theories about international relations. But this is not the case.

Political science is the systematic study of politics. Political scientists, like other social and natural scientists, have developed numerous methodologies to help us study politics and to better understand the complex political world we live in. But unlike people working in the natural sciences, political scientists cannot conduct laboratory experiments to isolate which circumstances produce specific outcomes. Every situation we study in political science is slightly different from the one we studied before. Yet political science research moves well beyond just describing the circumstances of isolated political events or social conditions to answering interesting questions about political change and political outcomes.

Most students have written many descriptive papers; in this text we focus instead on what we refer to as international relations research projects or original research studies at the college level. Descriptive papers (which often contain an argument or thesis) are generally explorations of topics or events. This type of paper expands personal knowledge but does not necessarily expand our general understanding of political phenomena or contribute *new* information. Original research studies at the college level increase our knowledge base about politics by examining very specific cases, events, and questions about political phenomena. You may think about the distinction between descriptive papers and original research studies as the difference between being well informed about a topic and being a scholar. It is about moving beyond the inquiry stage where you cultivate general knowledge about a topic to a stage where you can dissect a complex phenomenon, identify what scholars know and do not know about a topic, and judge the strength of various explanatory theories.

This may sound complicated, but it is not. You can construct an original research project—one that will broaden our understanding of international relations. Although this type of research takes time, planning, and patience, it can be intellectually stimulating and highly rewarding. The key to conducting research is to be systematic in your approach to studying an event or process and to place the conclusions reached from any individual research project within a broader context of what we already understand about politics. Our knowledge of international relations is based on the assembly of multiple pieces of information. Expanding knowledge is like putting together a puzzle; the outcomes of multiple studies are the pieces that collectively provide a larger picture of our political landscape. The ability to place a narrowly defined study that answers a specific question within a broader context of international relations scholarship is a distinguishing feature of research and a skill this book will help you learn.

Here is an example of what we are talking about when we suggest there are distinct differences between descriptive papers and original international relations research papers.

Topic for a descriptive paper:	Neotropical deforestation
Topic for a research paper:	What factors best explain differences in deforestation rates among the countries of Central America?

Notice in this example that the descriptive paper topic does not suggest any conclusion. It would yield only a topical overview, much like an encyclopedia entry. The college research paper requires not only reviewing the topic but also, more importantly, *answering a question* of interest to international relations scholars, students, and policy makers. To develop the college research paper, the researcher must first acquire general knowledge about the topic. This is why we often point out that original research at the college level begins at the point where most descriptive papers end.

When looking at the question posed in our example, you may ask, "Why focus the question so narrowly?" Why not ask, "What factors best explain differences in neotropical deforestation?" One reason is that the broader the question, the more difficult it is to answer with any specificity or confidence. Even though we would likely find some general explanations, conclusions from focused studies are often more reliable and, in the long run, more useful to understanding political behavior than an overly broad generalization of a broader topic that is not carefully and systematically explored. Think about how much more precisely you could answer this question if each person in your class looked at a different country and then you compared your findings. Your ability to draw an overall conclusion would ultimately be more reliable.

On occasion, criticism is lodged at research that is too narrowly focused—often suggesting that researchers may be losing track of the big picture by looking too closely at single events and phenomena. Granted, a single study is merely anecdotal unless it can be placed within a larger context of information. But focused studies provide the foundation for our broader understanding of politics. Think of it this way: natural scientists often repeat experiments over and over before developing theories about behavior. Repetition leads to greater confidence in a researcher's ability to theorize or predict future outcomes. Since international relations scholars cannot hold the same election over and over, or replicate a war, we must develop our theories and hypotheses about politics and political behavior by looking at research that is similar or related to our own inquiry. Only then can a single study be used to understand politics as a whole. This is why all good political science research builds on the work of others and why the research process described in this text teaches you how to conduct this type of research.

Whether we start with a narrow research question and explain how it fits within our broader understanding of international politics or start with a broad understanding of an area of international politics and narrow the focus to a single question, our research should augment the research completed by others. This book teaches you how to begin with a broad topic and then narrow your focus to a manageable level. It will help you develop a question of importance that will enhance our understanding in the field of international relations.

Every discipline has a distinctive set of conventions and practices that guides the structure of research within the field. The field of international relations is no different. While there are multiple approaches to research (e.g., qualitative, quantitative, case studies, etc.), there are several fundamental components to most international relations research papers. These components include a question designed to expand knowledge within the field (sometimes referred to as an original research question); connections to existing research (literature review); a description of the specific research approach used in the project (methodology); a section that discusses the systematic analysis of the data, evidence, or observations; and usually a summative conclusion.

Learning to conduct question-based research will forever make you think about international relations differently. Each time you put together a research project, you will better understand the complexity of political phenomena and the importance of looking beyond the obvious for causal explanations.

OVERVIEW OF PART I

Part I of this text explains how to conduct research and write a question-based research paper in international relations. It begins with a discussion of how to choose a topic and develop an initial research question and then moves through each step, including how to write the final paper.

Chapter 1 covers choosing a topic, developing a question, and understanding cause-and-effect relationships in international relations. Questions drive new research, and here we explain how to develop your own.

Chapter 2 covers how to place your research within a context. Conducting a literature review that covers how international relations scholars have studied your topic and what they have found is important in this process. This chapter explains how to find, read, and understand scholarly research in academic journals and other publications.

Chapter 3 sets out a framework or design for your research, explaining how a case-based approach works well for many students. The chapter suggests how to pick cases, how to use variables, and how to collect evidence or data in a systematic way.

Chapter 4 explains how to present your research in a written form. It gives suggestions for paper sections and examples as well.

Overall, Part I will guide you step by step in the process of writing an original international relations research paper.

Topic Selection and Question Development

Recently the *New York Times* published a number of articles on the Israeli–Palestinian conflict. Within them were descriptions of the most recent events occurring in this area of the world, each article grounded in rich historical detail. The journalists writing the articles provided readers with quotes from experts on Middle Eastern politics and the personal stories of individuals living in the region. They also included information about factors that precipitated intense periods of conflict and analysis of different conflict resolution scenarios. Although the articles presented by this internationally renowned newspaper provided a comprehensive summary of information on the politics of this conflict, the journalists who wrote these articles were not conducting political science research.

Political scientists ask a different set of questions than journalists and historians do. They ask questions that extend beyond the anecdotal circumstances of individual events, searching for linkages and distinctions among various cases, across time, regions, or subject areas. The goal for political scientists is to understand better events and political phenomena beyond isolated occurrences, thereby strengthening our ability to analyze political outcomes. Yet the study of politics is messy—no two events, conflicts, elections, treaties, or other political phenomena are ever exactly the same, making generalization about these occurrences challenging. Political scientists must build on the research of others, identifying common variables and anomalies among cases.

Many political scientists spend their entire careers researching and writing within a single topic area. International relations scholars, for example, study areas such as foreign policy, trade, war and conflict, international organizations, or sustainable development. The reason is that the depth of knowledge about a topic is directly related to one's ability to craft interesting questions. Developing a substantive knowledge base requires an investment of time and energy, but without such a base, it is difficult in international relations to develop a research paper beyond the thick description of a single event or circumstance. Therefore, many researchers find a topic of considerable interest to them and continue working within that area of research for years, thereby minimizing how much time is invested in just understanding the basic information needed to develop interesting research questions. Most students are used to writing descriptive papers but have little exposure to writing question-based research projects that require a substantive knowledge base. Yet this approach (question-based research) is typically the basis for college-level research in international relations.

This chapter will give you tips on how to choose and narrow a topic suitable for an IR project and how to break down the initial research process into a series of steps associated with the preliminary development of a question. Subsequent chapters will further describe the process that will ultimately outline how to develop fully a project that leads to a high-quality research paper in international relations.

CHOOSING A TOPIC

Choosing a topic is often the most difficult component of writing a research project. In some cases, professors assign topics for students to explore, thus minimizing the amount of time spent on this aspect of a project, but often students must select their own topics. Let us begin by assuming you can choose any general topic you wish for your research. This would leave you with nearly endless possibilities—after all, the focus of international relations is world affairs. Yet, if you are assigned a research paper early in the course, it is likely that you have limited prior knowledge about the course content. How do you pick a topic early in the term if this is the case?

Your textbook is your best resource for choosing a topic and building the foundational knowledge necessary for designing a research project. Even if your professor has not assigned any chapters yet, you can choose a topic by reviewing the list of thematic areas presented in your textbook. Important general topics such as the following themes in international relations are usually covered as individual chapters in your text.

International security	International political economy
Theories of power	Foreign policy
International conflict	Military force
Trade	International organizations and law
Currency and business	Integration
International development	North–South divisions

If you are in an upper-level course such as foreign policy or international political economy, you can use the same method to choose your topic. Look at the chapters for topics that seem particularly interesting to you. You can also go back to your introductory text for basic information.

Carefully focus on a single chapter. If you are interested in issues of war and the military, for example, read the chapter on international security or international conflict. If you are interested in the role of women in international relations, you may choose any chapter, but also include any sections on feminism and constructivism contained in your textbook. Table 1.1 sets out some common areas of interest for students and directs you to the most relevant chapters or sections found in many introductory IR texts.

Once you have read the full chapter, you should narrow your focus to a subtopic within the chapter. This will make the research process and question development easier in subsequent steps. For example, you may be interested in international conflict. A chapter on international conflict will probably include a number of different subtopics under the broad subtopic of conflicts of ideas, such as ethnic conflict, religious conflict, and ideological conflict. It may also include a discussion of competing theories or models that purport to explain components of international conflict. We suggest that you choose one

TABLE 1.1

Matching Areas of Interest with Text Chapters

Area of Interest	Focus of Chapter or Section
War in general, specific wars or conflicts, the military, terrorism, ethnic conflict, nationalism	Military force and/or international conflict, nationalism, global violence
International business, international trade	International political economy, trade, currency, corporate actors,
The differences among people's living conditions around the world, including issues related to poverty, income disparity, housing, education	North-South gap, international development, globalization
The role of women in IR	Any chapter, plus sections on women and IR, feminism, and constructivism
The United Nations or other international organizations	International organizations, inter-governmental actors
International agreements	International law, international organizations, international cooperation
Diplomacy	Foreign policy, international law
Human rights	International law, international organizations, international norms, nongovernmental actors, intergovernmental actors
Foreign policy decision making	Foreign policy
Mass media	Integration, globalization, foreign policy
Environment	Global environment

of these subtopics before conducting any research outside of your textbook discussion. Figure 1.1 illustrates the process of moving your focus from a topic to a subtopic to an even more narrow subtopic.

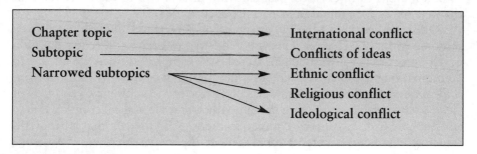

| FIGURE 1.1
| Narrowing Your Topic.

WRITING AN INITIAL SUBTOPIC QUESTION

The second step in developing a question-based research paper is to formulate a question associated with your subtopic choice. This question will later be refined to take into consideration the specific focus of your individual paper, but an initial question is needed to guide preliminary, foundation-building research.

Avoid questions that would result in projects that simply describe a process, an event, or terminology. For example, if your topic were trade and your subtopic global markets, you would want to avoid questions such as the following:

- "How do global markets operate?"
- "What is comparative advantage?"
- "Why do states use trade barriers?"
- "Which countries benefit the most from global markets?"

None of these questions would result in research papers that would contribute much more than would simple descriptive papers.

Interesting question-based research papers are most often those that require the researcher to explore variations between similar cases or variations over time for a single case. Such questions are interesting because, although no two cases are ever exactly the same, logic suggests these cases would continue to be highly similar, unless something notably different occurs or is introduced. After all, something must be different for outcomes to be different. When differences are noted among what are otherwise seemingly similar cases, the task of the researcher is to uncover the factors or variables that most likely explain the observed differences. From this respect, *question-based research papers seek to unravel the puzzles associated with not readily apparent cause-and-effect relationships.*

Here is an example of unraveling a cause-and-effect puzzle. A researcher observes that two countries with similar population levels and similar levels of arable land have vastly different levels of dependency on international food aid. One might ask, "What factors best explain variations in food aid dependency between these two countries of similar agricultural potential and level of population?" Note that the question asks for the best explanations for the observation. It is often outside the scope of a single research project to determine all the variables that might have some influence on the observed outcome. Therefore, one looks for the strongest explanatory variables, knowing (1) that change is complex and can be attributed to the interaction of more than one variable, and (2) that while some relationships appear plausible, they may indeed be false. The latter condition is referred to as a **spurious relationship** and is often difficult to identify. Yet identifying causal linkages and spurious connections is part of the process one goes through in trying to understand differences in political phenomena.

We suggest that you begin your research by developing a "what" question using your subtopic. Developing a "what" question will help you identify and research different variables. This type of question more easily leads you down a path of cause-and-effect exploration than do other types of questions that lead to descriptive papers. See Table 1.2 for examples.

TABLE 1.2

Developing Questions for Research

Topic	Subtopic	Inappropriate Subtopic Question	Appropriate Subtopic Question
International conflict: causes of war	Conflicts of interest: territorial disputes	"Where have territorial disputes occurred?" (This question would generate a list of places where disputes have occurred.)	"What factors most often explain territorial disputes among states?" (The question would generate specific factors that affect disputes most often.)
Trade: political economy	Markets	"Which nations benefit the most from expanding markets associated with international trade?" (This question would generate a list of nations that benefit the most from expanding markets.)	"What factors most often influence differences among nations in the exchange of goods and services in the international global market?" (This question would generate factors that most influence differences in the exchange of goods and services.)
The environment: inter-dependence	Natural resources	"When have nations fought over natural resources?" (This question would generate a list of dates.)	"Under what conditions will conflict arise among nation-states over natural resources?" (This question would generate the conditions that affect conflict.)

Note that each appropriate question asks what factors or conditions affect some aspect of the subtopic you are studying. Each appropriate question also has modifying terminology that reflects the complexity of world affairs and the fact that the research a political scientist would conduct to answer the question would result in generalizable rather than case-specific conclusions. Finally, the questions are crafted so that they focus on cause-and-effect relationships. The next step is to define variables.

MINIMIZE BIAS

At this stage, it is important to remember that high-quality research emerges from studies designed to minimize bias. Granted, all researchers are to some degree influenced by their personal values, experiences, and interests. But that is different from approaching research to prove a personal point or to convince others to believe as we do. You should design your research project to be as neutral as possible. In fact, research that uncovers the unpredicted is often the most interesting and valuable. More importantly, researchers who design a project hoping to get a desired outcome often fail to identify important explanatory variables. Do not make the mistake of beginning your research project by saying, "I want to prove that. . . ." There are many venues for writing personal opinion pieces and sharing your opinions on politics, but research papers should seek understanding and new information. After all, if you already know the answer, there is no reason to do the study.

DEFINING VARIABLES

Because the political world is dynamic and complex and no two political situations are ever exactly the same, we assume before beginning to answer a research question that multiple factors are likely responsible for shaping the circumstances and results we observe. Whether it is the reasons for the beginning of a war or the outcome of an election, several factors will be at play, some more important than others. It is the job of the researcher to figure out what factors shape what we observe and which ones are the most important.

Political scientists refer to the circumstances, topics, policies, or other phenomena that they want to understand as **dependent variables**. For example, if a researcher wants to understand why a policy failed, the study's dependent variable is the failure of the policy. If a researcher wants to understand why a particular country has suffered multiple military coups, the dependent variable of the research study is the occurrence of the country's multiple military coups. The factors believed to influence the project's dependent variable (i.e., to cause the dependent variable to undergo some form of change) are referred to as **independent variables**. See Figure 1.2 for a simple example of the relationship between dependent and independent variables. The presumed links between the dependent variable and independent variables are referred to as **hypotheses**.

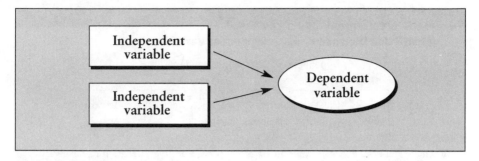

FIGURE 1.2
Relationship of Two Independent Variables to One Dependent Variable.

Understanding this research terminology is important. International relations research is often evaluated and discussed using the terms *dependent variable*, *independent variable*, and *hypotheses*. As you put together your research paper, you will encounter research that uses this language. Thus, we introduce these terms here and use them from this point forward. (Dependent and independent variables and the formation of hypotheses are discussed further in upcoming chapters.)

To develop a greater foundation for your research project and obtain a better understanding of dependent and independent variables, you can go back to your textbook once again. Reread the section associated with your research topic, but consciously think about your topic (the area of international relations that you want to know more about) as a dependent variable. Search the chapter for and create a list of what the author has identified as factors that shape your dependent variable. Then you can use this list of cause-and-effect relationships to develop hypotheses later about why chosen cases are different from one another or why a case may have changed over time. See Table 1.3 for examples of dependent and independent variables related to specific research questions.

RESEARCHING YOUR DEPENDENT VARIABLE BEYOND THE TEXTBOOK

Most of the research associated with a question-based research paper is focused on independent variables, but it is extremely important that you fully understand your dependent variable (your topic) *before* you begin your research and discussion of independent variables and hypotheses. Researching your dependent variable will likely be the same sort of research you have done in the past when writing descriptive papers, and you will likely use many of the same types of resources for this aspect of the research project, including encyclopedias, books, journals, newspapers, news magazines, and Internet and data resources. Gather as much general information about your dependent variable as possible so that you are familiar with historical trends and major areas of change and controversy.

> ### TABLE 1.3
>
> **Identifying Dependent and Independent Variables**
>
> | Research Question | Dependent Variable | Independent Variables (IVs) |
> |---|---|---|
> | "What factors most often explain territorial disputes among states?" | Existence of territorial disputes | Factors contributing to territorial disputes:
IV1: Irredentism
IV2: Forcible alteration of borders by militarily strong nation-states
IV3: Ethnic secession efforts
IV4: Lingering historical disputes
IV5: Ill-defined nonland boundaries (air and water borders) |
> | "What factors most often influence differences among nations in the exchange of goods and services in the international global market?" | Level of trade in goods and services | Factors contributing to higher rates of international trade for some states and lower rates for others:
IV1: Resource availability
IV2: Workforce education levels
IV3: Internal market structures
IV4: Trade barriers |

At this stage, you are concentrating on general information about your dependent variable. One good hint is to make sure that you take notes on how your textbook and other sources define your area of interest. For example, if you are interested in ethnic conflict, it is important to know that ethnic conflict is defined as conflict between "large groups of people who share ancestral, language, cultural, or religious ties and a common identity" (Goldstein 2003, p. 545).

The time you spend to understand your dependent variable will be well worth your effort as your project evolves. You will know that you are well along when you can tell your roommate a good deal about the history, definitions, trends, and major examples of your topic. It may help to think of all the information you have gathered about your dependent variable as the material you might have used for a descriptive paper.

See the box for examples of the types of background information you might gather on the dependent variable at this stage of the research process. Keep in mind that this is only a preliminary list of questions you might use to begin researching the dependent variables listed.

For a question-based research paper, you will have to go further with your research. After completing your general research on your dependent variable, you will be ready to move to the next stage of the research process. In this second stage, you will conduct a literature review—a defining feature of college-level and professional scholarship. You will learn how to do this in Chapter 2.

SUGGESTED QUESTIONS FOR DEPENDENT VARIABLE RESEARCH

Dependent Variable: Territorial Disputes

- What is the definition of a territorial dispute?
- Have territorial disputes been increasing or decreasing in the last century?
- Have territorial disputes been occurring in some parts of the world more than others?
- Which disputes have lasted the longest during the last century?
- Have any disputes resulted in significant casualties or large-scale wars?
- How might one define a major conflict versus a minor conflict?
- How have countries around the world reacted to territorial disputes?

Dependent Variable: Trade in Goods and Services

- What is the definition of trade, goods, and services?
- How are the goods and services traded internationally categorized?
- Which countries are large importers of finished goods?
- Which countries are large importers of natural resources?
- Which countries have significant levels of trade in services?
- Which countries purchase services internationally?
- Has the level of trade among states been increasing or decreasing over time?
- Do all countries benefit from international trade in goods and services?
- What role do multinational corporations play in international trade?
- What international organizations address issues of international trade?
- What international agreements have shaped international trade?
- What areas of trade affect women differently than men?

Dependent Variable: Natural Resource Conflicts

- What is the definition of natural resource conflicts?
- What natural resources have been objects of conflicts in the last fifty years?
- Currently, what natural resource conflicts exist and where?
- What international agreements exist to mediate natural resource conflicts?
- When have natural resource conflicts become violent?

Dependent Variable: Revolutionary Movements

- What is the definition of a revolutionary movement?
- Where have there been revolutionary movements?
- How long do revolutionary movements generally last?
- What range of outcomes is associated with revolutionary movements?

FREQUENTLY ASKED QUESTIONS

"I have no idea what topic to pick for my research paper. What should I do?"

- Think about what topics or issues are important to you. Then look for a connection to international relations.
- Talk to friends or family about what interests them.
- Read the newspaper to get a sense of important and interesting current issues.

"My topic seems too narrow. What should I do?"

- Think about how you would characterize your topic. In what chapter or under what section would you place it in your textbook? This will give you an idea about how to make your topic broader.
- Think about your topic as a concept (e.g., military conflicts involving superpowers) rather than as a specific event (the Vietnam War) or as something occurring within a specific country (the 1979 Soviet invasion of Afghanistan).

"My topic seems too broad. What should I do?"

- Think about what aspects of the broader topic interest you. Why do you find the topic fascinating? This can lead you to a narrower subtopic.
- Think about the details associated with your broad topic. For example, if you are interested in military conflict, are you interested in the onset, the duration, or the resolution of the conflict?

EXERCISES FOR CHAPTER 1

1. Choose a broad topic and make a list of potential subtopics.
2. Choose a subtopic and develop a "what" question.
3. Choose a subtopic and make a list of independent variables found in your text that may affect your dependent variable.
4. Develop a list of descriptive questions about your dependent variable that can be answered through general research.

Scholarly Literature and the Literature Review

This text is designed as an introduction to writing a question-based research paper with a format much like research papers published in the field of international relations. Once you have chosen a topic and developed a question, the next stage in developing your question-based research project is to expand your research to include international relations scholarship.

International relations scholarship consists of published studies of political phenomena *by scholars*. This form of information is quite different from the types of information you obtain from newspapers, encyclopedias, magazines, and websites (sources used to learn more general information about your dependent variable). These utilize the research of others, but the authors of such works do not personally design systematic studies to investigate specific questions. They provide primarily general, descriptive information that sometimes incorporates the findings from IR studies, but they do not conduct the studies themselves. Much of IR scholarship describes primary research and learned conclusions reached by scholars investigating specific research questions.

It is important to incorporate scholarship into research papers for two main reasons. First, question-based research projects include many of the elements and processes used by researchers in the field of international relations. Incorporating scholarship into formal research papers is a standard within the field. Most scholars who engage in formal research reference the work of other scholars when writing up their own findings. They do so because the goal is to build knowledge of political phenomena. This is accomplished by establishing links between various research projects, thereby creating an ongoing accumulation of knowledge established one study at a time. Including a section devoted to the findings of other researchers will clearly distinguish your project as one grounded in knowledge of the discipline and one with appropriate international relations methodology.

The second reason to include the findings of other researchers is that reading the scholarly literature will assist you in refining your specific projects and identifying possible independent variables and hypotheses (or tentative explanations of the relationship between variables). The scholarly literature is much like a conversation among those working in the field. Researchers share their work through their publications rather than through spoken conversations. Scholars learn from one another by reading each others' work. Researchers carefully document how they conduct their research and reach their conclusions. This facilitates the use of their findings by other researchers who wish to do similar research on new cases or create studies that expand on interesting findings. Thus, researching the scholarly literature will help you shape your research question, identify independent variables and/or theories to explore in your own question-based project, and eventually formulate explanatory hypotheses.

This chapter will teach you how to identify the types of resources that qualify as scholarly publications, how to find them, and how to best use scholarship to shape your specific project.

TERMINOLOGY

Social scientists refer to published scholarship as **literature**. The process of reading and reviewing published scholarship in the field is referred to as a **review of the literature**. This phrase is commonly shortened simply to **literature review**. When academics talk about **conducting a literature review**, they are talking about researching (reviewing) the scholarly literature. When they talk about **writing a literature review**, they are talking about writing a summary of such research. Because this is the most commonly used terminology in the field for this type of research, we will use these terms as we discuss this aspect of research and writing from this point forward.

GETTING STARTED ON YOUR LITERATURE REVIEW

When you start your literature review, you will be looking for *scholarly studies* by other researchers primarily associated with your project's *dependent* variable. This is important because many of the sources you may have used previously for research papers may not be appropriate for a literature review. Remember the purpose served by the literature review. You need it to ground your study in the field of international relations, and you will use it to better understand what other researchers understand. When written up, your literature review will *describe research*, not tell a story.

First and foremost, remember: all resources are not created equal! Today's world of technology has opened up avenues for an unprecedented exchange of information. Tens of thousands of publishers around the world are producing books, journals, magazines, and newspapers, some of which have extremely high standards for accuracy; other companies will publish anything for a fee. You need only read the headlines of a tabloid magazine to know that just because something is in print does not mean that the information printed is reliable or even truthful.

Judging the reliability of sources on the World Wide Web can be especially difficult. It costs little or nothing to maintain a website, and there is no independent review process for judging the quality of various materials on the Web or for granting a site address. Therefore, you can find websites maintained by the world's leading scientific research organizations as well as websites maintained by individuals who still believe that the earth is flat.

Your literature review should focus on **scholarly resources**—resources considered to be highly reliable by academic scholars and research professionals in the field of international relations. The types of resources most often used for the literature review in IR research papers include printed materials such as books, journal articles, and other published studies that have been subjected to peer review. These resources can be found in both hard copy and electronic forms and are not always easily distinguishable from less reliable resources. We discuss types of resources in the following subsections.

PEER REVIEW: ALL INFORMATION IS NOT CREATED EQUAL

Peer review is the process by which research is reviewed for accuracy by other experts prior to publication. The peer-review process is designed to ensure that published research meets the highest standards of the discipline. To minimize bias, most reviews are blind, which means that the reviewers do not know whose work they are reading. Reviewers assess the author's literature review to make sure no important studies have been overlooked. Reviewers scrutinize the methodology used for the project, often rechecking calculations and evaluating data sources. After review, authors must amend their studies to the satisfaction of the journal's editorial board. Submitted studies that are found by reviewers to have too many inaccuracies or that fail to meet the standards of the editorial board are refused publication.

Scholarly Journals

Scholarly journals are the most important sources for literature reviews, and information from them should comprise the bulk of materials discussed in your literature review. These journals are the first place that academics turn to find the most topic-specific information available when they begin their research projects. Scholarly journals target an audience of academics, professionals, and students within various fields and professions. Here is a brief list of IR journals.

American Journal of International Law	International Relations
British Journal of International Studies	International Security
Conflict Management and Peace Studies	International Studies
Conflict Studies	International Studies Quarterly
Cooperation and Conflict	Journal of Conflict Resolution
Harvard International Journal of Press/Politics	Journal of International Affairs
International Affairs	Journal of Peace Research
International Organization	World Politics
International Political Science Review	

Merely having the word "Journal" in the title does not necessarily qualify a publication as a *scholarly* journal. Some magazines and industry publications call themselves journals but do not fall into the category of scholarly journals. This is not to say that the information in these magazines and industry publications is inaccurate. To the contrary, many such publications provide valuable and reliable information. But these publications target a general or nonacademic audience. Their presentation of material is often one-dimensional, and they often provide discussion in nontechnical language, generally writing about the findings of other researchers rather than publishing actual research studies.

REPUTABLE JOURNALS OF COMMENTARY AND CURRENT AFFAIRS

A number of highly respected academic journals publish articles of commentary and analysis of current affairs but do not follow the research format of scholarly journal articles. Examples are the widely read journals *Foreign Affairs* and *Foreign Policy*. Information in these journals is reliable but atypical in format compared to research journals. Because journals of commentary do not follow the approach to research discussed in this text, we encourage you to ask your professor whether articles from this type of journal are acceptable in your literature reviews.

Today, many college libraries no longer carry as many hard copies of journals as they once did. Many journal subscriptions are purchased in electronic form and can be accessed through large databases along with other materials. The availability of online journals enables several students to access the same journal article at one time. Online availability also allows students to access articles using their personal computers in their dorm rooms and during hours when libraries are closed. But there are drawbacks to relying on online journal research.

One drawback is that there may be a blackout period associated with the journal online. This means that your online search result may be restricted to articles published one year or more ago. A second drawback of online journal searches is that unless you are familiar with the journal (e.g., it is on the list presented earlier or your professor or research librarian has verified its classi-fication), it is often difficult to distinguish whether an article you obtain electronically is from a scholarly journal. When you use hard copies of jour-nals, it is much easier to tell. Often search engines group academic journals, newspapers, magazines, and industry publications under the heading of schol-arly resources. Yet generally, political scientists consider only academic jour-nals to fall into the category of sources most appropriate for literature reviews. If your professor indicates that your literature review should contain primarily peer-reviewed sources or scholarly journals, you should *not* rely on search engines to make the decision about what is and is not such a scholarly resource. Here are some tips to help you determine whether an online article comes from a scholarly journal.

- **Level of detail:** A scholarly journal should provide you with more detail than the general information contained in a newspaper or magazine article.
- **Level of discourse:** Journal articles are written in technical language. Nonscholarly resources are written for a general audience.
- **Structure:** Most journal articles contain an abstract with the paper's thesis, an introduction, a literature review, and a discussion of the methods used to draw conclusions. Sources of information will be cited. In general, you will not find an abstract or a literature review (direct references to other scholarly studies) in a nonscholarly publication.
- **Explanation of methodology:** Journal articles explain the methods used to analyze evidence and/or data and indicate which resources were used to draw conclusions.
- **Footnotes and endnotes:** Most international relations journal articles suitable for literature reviews contain footnotes or endnotes.
- **Bibliography:** Scholarly journal articles contain a bibliography or refer-ence list. Magazines and newspapers rarely do. Trade publications seldom contain them.
- **Date of publication:** Scholarly journals are usually published monthly, quarterly, or biannually and usually have a volume or issue number coinciding with the time of year released. Newspapers and magazines are usually published daily, weekly, or monthly.

IDENTIFYING SCHOLARLY JOURNALS

If you are unsure whether or not a publication in hard copy would be considered a scholarly journal, look for these features of scholarly publications.

- Most scholarly journals limit advertising to only ads from other publishers.
- Near the front of a scholarly publication is a list of editorial board advisors (most of whom have university affiliations), along with publication standards.
- Pagination continues from one issue of a journal to the next issue.
- Volume numbers are used to identify each year of the publication.

Peer-Reviewed Books

Books about politics are some of the most widely purchased nonfiction books available in bookstores today. You should be careful, however, about the decision to include books in the literature review section of your research paper. Many of the books you find in popular bookstores are written for a general audience and contain interesting information about politics, but because they do not discuss specific studies, they often are not suitable for inclusion (remember, your task when conducting your literature review is to evaluate *research* on your topic, not information that builds general knowledge). The inclusion of books in your literature review must also be done carefully because not all books on political topics go through the process of academic peer review. Books subjected to critical peer reviews before publication are appropriate for inclusion in your literature review but figuring out whether a book has gone through such a review requires scrutiny.

In general, college and university libraries are generally careful about the types of books selected for their collections favoring peer-reviewed publications over those that are not. Peer-reviewed books can be used in literature reviews but the information in any book must be carefully assessed as most books are written with multiple audiences in mind. You can also draw some conclusions about whether a book is peer reviewed by considering who published it. University presses, as well as many other reputable publishers, follow academic standards for peer review. College or university libraries often limit their selections to this type of publisher. If in doubt, check with your university librarian or your professor to help you assess whether a particular book would be a suitable resource for your literature review.

Should you decide to use a book in your literature review you will need to determine if the thesis of the book aligns with your dependent variable, keeping in mind that you should not be using book information in your literature review the same way you use book information in your introduction or for background information. Should you choose to include peer-reviewed books in your literature review, it is best to choose those that thematically align with your dependent variable.

Edited Books

One type of book with which you may not be familiar is the edited book composed of work by numerous authors. The same standards for books by a single author apply to these edited books but edited books are often more useful in literature reviews than monographs. One reason is that few edited books in international relations are published for a general audience. This means that you will not have to sift through the volume to find the information relevant to your research project. Secondly, edited books found in university and college libraries generally have undergone some form of peer review prior to publication. And finally, edited books are thematic with an interconnection among the chapters. This means you will likely find many chapters in a single book that will apply to your project. Do not hesitate to reference several or all chapters from an edited book in your literature review. (See Chapter 11 for how to cite a chapter within an edited book.)

Electronic Sources

Most college libraries have large databases available online where you can access academic resources electronically. These databases provide resources that are different from information that you access through any commercial Internet search engine. If you use electronic resources not associated with your university library, you should be extremely careful in determining the reliability of these resources. Although you will find an abundance of information on the Internet that may apply to your research project, resources found online are generally not suitable literature review sources. Information from organizations should not be included in the literature review for your study. This is primarily because most organizations post data or research summaries but not the actual studies themselves, and much of the research posted on organizations' websites has not been subjected to the peer-review process. Stick to the actual write-ups of studies by other scholars for your literature review.

HOW TO SEARCH THE LITERATURE

Few scholarly journal articles can be found through the popular, public Internet search engines such as Google, Yahoo!, and AltaVista, although you may have some luck with Google Scholar. You are more likely to locate the types of journal articles best suited for a college-level research project by using the databases and reference books available through your institution's library or through a research **gateway**—a link to another academic site that has additional resources usually organized by research area or topic. (The next subsection lists some helpful IR gateways.) You can find books in a similar way.

Finding Scholarly Journal Articles

Most college or university libraries now provide access to indexes in electronic form online. The first thing you should do when looking for suitable sources is to familiarize yourself with your library's home page and look at the databases or indexes available to you. If you cannot find any or don't know where to look, ask the reference librarian for help. Specifically, you want to find those databases that will guide you to scholarly articles and information in the social sciences because political science and international relations are classified as social sciences. JSTOR is a very popular research database that allows you to search by discipline and obtain full-text copies of the scholarly articles you find. If you have access to JSTOR, begin your search for sources for your literature review there. You can click on a box (under advanced searching) to limit your search to only political science journals.

If you do not have access to JSTOR, you can start with another academic search database. Examples include EBSCOhost, INFOTRAC, and ProQuest.

Your reference librarian or professor can suggest alternative databases to start your search. Most academic search engines also allow you to limit your search to refereed or scholarly journals. For example, in EBSCOhost you can click on the box marked "peer reviewed," in ProQuest you can click on the box marked "show articles from peer reviewed publications only," and in INFO-TRAC you can click on the box marked "to refereed publications." But remember that these methods for filtering articles are not foolproof. You will still need to use the criteria discussed earlier to scrutinize the articles that emerge with a computer search to determine their utility.

If you are having trouble narrowing the number of hits you are getting, try searching only one journal at a time or restricting by date. Some colleges and universities give you access to Journal Finder, which allows you to type in the name of a journal and obtain information on how to access full-text copies of articles. After you find ways to access a particular journal, another strategy is to search through the table of contents of recent volumes to find articles related to your dependent variable.

Once you identify indexes and databases, the key to efficient searching is tied to your ability to understand the subtopic areas of your research. For instance, plugging in the search word "international conflict" will get you thousands of articles. Modifying your search to "ethnic conflict" will get you fewer, but modifying to "ethnic relations—political aspects" will get you a manageable number. See the box about online searches for some tips. One of the most important ideas is to use the reference books in your library that list the Library of Congress subject headings. You can look up your topic and find a list of search terms that will help you immensely.

KEEPING AN ONLINE SEARCH MANAGEABLE

Search Subtopics, Not Topics

General topics will always return more citations than you could possibly want. Before starting your search, identify a number of subtopics related to your research interest.

Limit Subtopics by Discipline and Dates

If a subtopic search yields far too many articles, limit your search to that subtopic, but modify your search by looking at articles only from international relations journals. You can also try limiting your subtopic search to a ten-year period and reducing the number of years depending on how many articles are found.

Search by Library of Congress Headings

Libraries have reference books listing the Library of Congress subject headings. Searching under a subject heading related to your topic is crucial to finding useful information.

Use Boolean Operators

Boolean operators are simply words used to modify your topic to make your online search more specific to your needs. Most search engines use some Boolean operators but not necessarily all of them. Here is a list of the major operators.

- **AND**: When used between search terms, this operator tells the computer that both terms must apply to the articles returned by the search.
- **OR**: This operator usually increases the number of articles you get in a search because it tells the computer you would be happy with articles discussing either one of the topic keywords that the OR sits between. It can be helpful if a topic is sometimes discussed under different titles, such as "global warming" or "climate change."
- **NOT**: This helps you narrow a search to a subtopic when one group of articles dominates another. For example, most articles you will find on campaign finance are associated with campaign finance reform. If you want articles on campaign finance but not on reform, indicate this with an operator: "campaign finance NOT reform."
- *****: Not all search engines allow the asterisk operator, but if your search engine does, it can be very handy. The asterisk operator tells the computer to search for articles with any derivative of the word that contains the asterisk. For example, using the search word "enviro*," you would find articles containing the words environ, environment, environmental, environmentalist, environmentally. As another example, you can locate the following terms in articles by using the search term "wom*": woman, women, woman's, women's, womanly.
- **NEAR**: This operator is especially helpful for narrowing your search when your topic includes commonly used words such as "climate change." You could search using "climate AND change," but that would not necessarily get you articles on global climate change. Rather, you would get articles on climate with a reference somewhere in the article to the word "change," but they could be totally unrelated to climate change. By using "climate NEAR change" you will get articles where these words are probably used in the same sentence. This is far more likely to give you the type of articles you want.

One other way to search for scholarly literature on your topic is by going through gateways, which are basically electronic portholes into the resources available through many of the nation's largest research institutions. Here's a list of some gateways that provide resources useful to international relations research.

- http://wsrv.clas.virginia.edu/~rjb3v/rjb.html
  Foreign Affairs Online lists a broad range of sources for the study of international relations.

- http://mitpress.mit.edu/journals/INOR/deibert-guide/TOC.html
  Ronald J. Deibert's site, Virtual Resources: International Relations
  Research Resources on the Web, contains subject links including human
  rights, international political economy, nongovernmental organizations
  and activists, and international security, among others.

- http://guides.lib.umich.edu/content.php?pid=17084&sid=115547
  This University of Michigan site contains a list to IR sites.

- http://guides.lib.umich.edu/content.php?pid=26817
  This is the University of Michigan's site on international organizations.

- http://www.policyarchive.org/
  Policy Archive is a digital library that contains public policy research
  conducted by scholars and think-tanks.

Although you may have difficulty accessing the full text of the articles you
find online, many of these articles will be available in hard copy through your
college or university library, and if you begin your broad literature review
early in your project development, you can obtain just about any article you
find. Many libraries also have interlibrary loan (ILL) services that for little or
no fee will send you copies of journal articles not available at your institution.
This type of service, however, often takes a couple of weeks. To take advantage of ILL services, you must start your literature review long before your
paper's due date.

Literature review searches are nonlinear. There is no specific path for finding sources related to your topic. One reason is that many scholarly journals
have overlapping themes. For example, ethnic conflict could just as easily fall
within the publishing guidelines of a journal covering international law as it
could be found in a journal on international organizations. Therefore, we cannot give you specific roadmaps that can easily take you to all the articles you
will need for your literature review. But we can give you some tips.

The best advice for conducting your research on the scholarly literature
review is to rely on the work of others as your guide. For the literature review,
begin by conducting a search using standard search techniques, with the initial goal of finding a journal article that is very closely related to your broad
topic—through JSTOR, for example. If you find an article that is closely related, you can employ techniques that will help you find additional resources
through what we call backward mapping and forward mapping.

- **Backward mapping:** Most journal articles are heavily weighted with
  references to other authors' works. This practice of giving credit to all
  related studies and carefully documenting the sources of information can
  be used to help you find the information you need. To backward map,
  find one good journal article closely related to your study. This article
  will have its own literature review and a bibliography of sources. Use
  the bibliography from this article as your search guide. Follow up on all

sources that appear related to your dependent variable. The articles you find using this article can then be used for additional backward mapping to find more articles.

- **Forward mapping:** You can get a good idea of a given article's importance to the field of international relations by using the *Social Sciences Citation Index*. This resource will provide you with a list of scholarly sources that cite a particular article. This is important in determining the current value of a study or theory that may be fairly old. If scholars continue to cite a work many years or even decades after its initial publication, it is likely to be a seminal article with valuable information that you should include in your literature review. Forward mapping will also help you find additional sources by identifying other studies related to the same article. The *Social Sciences Citation Index* is available either in hard copy or online. If you have questions about how to use the *Social Sciences Citation Index*, you should ask the reference librarian.

While you can access a good number of journals online in full-text form, in some cases an abstract will be available but not the entire article. Citing an abstract is insufficient. You will need to obtain a full copy of the article if you include it in your research paper and should cite information found in the article itself, not just the abstract. *Do not limit your literature review to only articles that can be accessed online.* There is also great utility in viewing the entire journal in which you find a valuable article. Many journals have entire issues focused on a single topic, which may lead you to related articles that did not show up in your original search. You may find interesting journal articles by going to the current periodicals section of your library and looking at the hard copy versions of recently published journals. (Again, refer to the list presented earlier in this chapter for titles of some IR publications.)

Searching for Scholarly Books

Although the bulk of your literature review will be conducted by reading scholarly journal articles, you should also look for scholarly books on your topic. The first place to start is your university or college library's catalog to discover which books are available where you are. Second, some libraries maintain cooperative agreements with other area libraries so that you may be able to order books from these libraries via your library website. Finally, as mentioned earlier, almost all college and university libraries participate in broader ILL arrangements. Through ILL you can order books that are not in your own library but can be sent to you in a matter of days or a few weeks. To find books that you may want to order via ILL, you can use WorldCat, which many university libraries have access to online. Search via WorldCat, note the citations you are interested in, and order these works through ILL if they're unavailable in your own library. Make sure you understand any restrictions on ILL at your institution. Sometimes there are restrictions on the number of books you can order via ILL, for example.

USING A REVIEW OF THE LITERATURE TO SHAPE YOUR PROJECT

As you begin your search in the IR literature, you will quickly see whether or not you need to narrow your "what" question or broad topic. Some topics in international relations have been studied far more than others. For instance, the topic of ethnic conflict has been widely studied, and if you plug this topic into a search engine, you will get far more articles than you will have time to read and far more than necessary for inclusion. In contrast, if your topic is women and guerrilla war, you will find fewer related research articles. Your course professor will likely establish the number of articles you should include in your literature review. If you have a topic on which there is little published scholarship available, perhaps only a dozen articles, the decision about which articles to choose becomes easy. You discuss them all. But if you have chosen a topic on which there is a vast amount of published research (dozens of articles), you will need to narrow the focus of your topic to a particular aspect. Deciding how to narrow a topic may be a bit overwhelming when there are fifty articles on your topic and your professor asked you to choose only a dozen.

One way to think about a literature review is to think of it as a description of a conversation taking place among scholars—written communication about individual research projects. Imagine scholars getting together to discuss their work in person. If you invited scholars writing about women and guerilla war to attend a meeting, you could probably fit all the scholars in a relatively small room for a face-to-face conversation. Yet if everyone writing on the topic of ethnic conflict were to attend such a meeting, there would be so many scholars present that you would need a large room, and the conversation likely would be so diverse that scholars would self-divide into groups, with scholars entering into discussions with other scholars who conduct similar research.

Taking this analogy a bit further, in a room full of scholars who study ethnic conflict, you might find a group discussing how conflicts begin. Another group may be involved in a lengthy discussion of the factors that explain why ethnic conflicts last for a short period of time or a long period of time. A third group may be arguing about the conditions under which third-party intervention will increase the likelihood of conflict resolution. A fourth group may be discussing particular types of ethnic conflict. A fifth group may be focusing on different theoretical lenses covered (e.g., realism, idealism, or constructivism) and explanations of ethnic conflict. These are all conversations about ethnic conflict, but they are sublevel conversations about specific aspects of the topic.

Within these sublevel conversations, you would find that scholars study similar but seldom the same cases. For instance, of those discussing how conflicts begin, some would talk about research they did on the origination of ethnic conflicts in Africa, while others might discuss the origination of ethnic conflicts in Europe. Others might have conducted studies comparing the origin of conflict when groups are of different sizes. In other words, the scholars would discuss different cases, but all the studies they discuss would be related in some way.

A literature review for a question-based research paper describes the conversation that would take place among scholars who have conducted research related to your topic. If you have chosen a topic that has not been studied much, the conversation will be small, and you should describe this entire conversation in your paper. If you have chosen a topic that is widely studied, there will be many, many articles on the topic, representing a conversation among scholars in which many sublevel conversations are taking place. To make both your project and your literature review manageable, you should narrow your research question so that it ties into one of the sublevel conversations. For instance, if you began with "What factors explain ethnic conflicts?" you would need to narrow the focus of your question to reflect a sublevel discussion and then choose resources from your search efforts that are related to your new, narrower question. See Figure 2.1 for examples.

Because journal articles will be your most important and useful resource for your literature review, we discuss them a bit further in the next section.

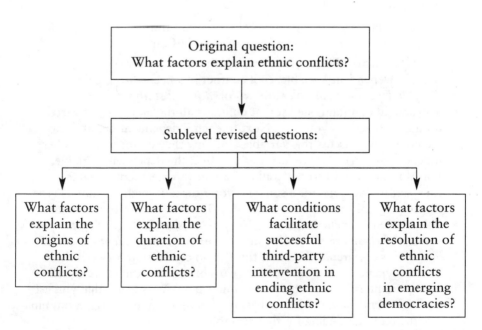

FIGURE 2.1
Narrowing a Research Question to Fit the Literature.

HOW TO READ A SCHOLARLY JOURNAL ARTICLES

Scholarly journals are written specifically for academics, which means the language used in these journals is often more technical than what is typically found in newspapers and magazines. Do not be put off by this. Even though you may not understand the more sophisticated mathematical equations or regression tables sometimes found in scholarly articles, you do have the skills to identify the question(s) being asked by the authors, the variables they are interested in, and the findings they present. When you sit down with a journal article, first find the answers to the following questions.

- *With what research question did the author(s) start the study?*
  This may not be clearly stated but will be implied in the abstract or the introduction. Sometimes you might need to read the author's literature review to figure this out, but usually you can determine the question in the early pages of the publication. We suggest that you try and write out the study's question in a "what format:"
  What factors affect . . .?
  Under what conditions does . . . affect . . .?
- *What is the study's dependent variable?*
  Once you figure out the research question, you will know the dependent variable. Make sure that you take notes on how the author defines the dependent variable (remember: the dependent variable is what the study seeks to understand).
  Examples:
  What factors best explain voter turnout in Iraq?
      Dependent Variable: voter turnout in Iraq

  What factors best explain civil conflict in Chechnya?
      Dependent Variable: civil conflict in Chechnya?
- *What independent variables are explored in the study?*
  You should maintain one list that contains all the independent variables found in all articles you read. Next to each independent variable, note which authors discuss this variable and how they define it (remember: independent variables are factors that affect the dependent variable. For example, voter turnout could be a study's dependent variable. Independent variables for a study on voter turnout might include 1) type of campaign, 2) weather on voting day 3), voter registration changes)
- *What general conclusions did the researcher(s) reach regarding the connection between the study's dependent and independent variables?*
  Sometimes researchers find that there is no connection between the chosen dependent and independent variables. Such results are equally as important as findings that show connections. We suggest that you list each independent variable and beside each independent variable, summarize the research finding for that variable.

To provide some examples of this process, we read three IR journal articles and identified our answers to these questions; see the box about searching for variables.

Example 1

Hemmer, Christopher, and Peter J. Katzenstein. 2002. Why is there no NATO in Asia? Collective identity, regionalism, and the origins of multinationalism. *International Organization* 56 (Summer): 575–607.

- **The "what" question:** What factors shape the structure of security arrangements between the United States and Southeast Asia?
- **The dependent and independent variables:**
    - DV: The U.S. choice of bilateral (rather than multilateral) security arrangements
    - IV1: Great power status
    - IV2: Desire for efficient responses to threats
    - IV3: Regional identity
- **The conclusion/thesis:** The United States saw Southeast Asia as part of an alien political community and chose bilateral security arrangements because of the United States' great power status, desire for efficient responses to threats, and regional identity in the 1940s and 1950s.

Example 2

Liberman, Peter. 2001. The rise and fall of the South African bomb. *International Security* 26 (Fall): 45–87.

- **The "what" question:** What factors led to the South African decision to dismantle its nuclear weapons program in 1990–1991?
- **The dependent and independent variables:**
    - DV: South Africa's decision to dismantle its nuclear weapons program
    - IV1: Security incentives
    - IV2: Organizational politics
    - IV3: International pressure
- **The conclusion/thesis:** South Africa's decision to dismantle its nuclear weapons program in 1990–1991, after its building of such weapons in the 1970s and 1980s, was influenced by security incentives, organizational politics, and international pressure.

Example 3

Press, Daryl G. 2001. The myth of air power in the Persian Gulf War and the future of warfare. *International Security* 26 (Fall): 5–45.

- **The "what" question:** What factors explain the U.S. and British victory in the first Gulf War?
- **The dependent and independent variables:**
    - DV: U.S. and British Gulf War Victory
    - IV1: Air power
    - IV2: Superiority of coalition ground troops
    - IV3: Iraqi poor timing
- **The conclusion/thesis:** Air power was "neither sufficient nor necessary" in the U.S. and British victory in the first Gulf War, as the superiority of coalition ground troops and poor timing greatly affected the victory.

Note how systematically the information from the journal articles examined in the above examples is documented. For each journal article, you need to note the full citation, the research question, the dependent variable, each independent variable the authors addressed, and the study's findings for these variables. We suggest that you place the information from each journal article on separate pieces of paper or on separate note cards. This will allow you to group, match, and decide how best to discuss various articles when the time comes to write the literature review section of your own paper. You should also consider using this method for other sources under consideration for your review as well (i.e. edited book chapters, peer-reviewed books).

How do you know when you are finished with your research in the scholarly literature? Unfortunately, there is no good answer to this question. In general, you are well along in your research when you begin to recognize the names of authors and can group your sources by subtopics and independent variables.

Your course instructor will likely provide you with guidelines for how many sources she or he wants you to include in your project. Your professor may even want you to limit your search to selected journals. Therefore, we suggest that you clarify this aspect of your paper with your professor. If the number of sources in your literature review is up to you, remember that literature research is only one part of your project, so you should budget your time wisely. We suggest that approximately one-third of the time you devote to your project should be spent developing your literature review. The next chapter describes how to choose the case or cases for your paper and how to collect evidence about your case(s).

FREQUENTLY ASKED QUESTIONS

"I am having difficulty finding enough journal articles for my literature review. What should I do?"

- Every article you find has the potential to lead you to dozens of other articles. Take one of the articles you have found and identify through its citations other journal articles.
- Plug your dependent variable into the *Social Sciences Citation Index* as a search term or search phrase.
- Many journals publish volumes by theme. Use Journal Finder to locate a specific journal that you know has published at least one article on your topic. Open volumes within that journal and read the titles and/or abstracts from each issue. If you find a title that looks like it matches, find the article and use it to backward and forward map.
- Authors often publish in the same area of research for many years. Search for other articles by the author of one of the articles you have already found.

"I found too many articles. How do I know which ones to use and which ones not to use?"

- Stick to articles that are most closely related to your specific research question.
- Divide your articles into groups according to common variables, common methodologies, time period, and so on. Then limit your choice of articles to one to three groups, depending on how many articles your professor would like you to use.
- Focus on articles that discuss independent variables that you would like to explore in your study.

■ The number of times an article is cited by other scholars is considered one measure of an article's importance to the field. If you have too many articles, use the *Social Sciences Citation Index* to see how many times each article has been cited by others. You may then want to select only (or most) of your articles based on the number of times the article has been cited by other scholars.

"Some articles contain mathematical equations and tables that I do not understand. How should I approach these?"

■ Recognize that you can identify and understand the research question, variables, and conclusions even if the math is above your level. Authors use words as well as numbers.

■ Some terms are easy to understand.

   ■ **Large-n study** means that the number of cases is large and suitable for quantitative (or statistical) analysis.

   ■ **Models** attempt to simplify our understanding of how variables relate to each other. Scholars can then use a large number of cases to test the soundness of those models.

   ■ A **significant** result in a statistical analysis means that a result is not likely to have occurred by chance. Most large-n studies are concerned with the **level of significance**. Common levels are 10 percent, 5 percent, and 1 percent. For example, a level of 1 percent means there is a 1 percent possibility that the result is due to chance. The lower the significance level, the stronger the relationship. You may see such text as "$*p < .1$, $**p < .05$, $***p < .01$" at the bottom of some tables. The asterisks next to numbers in the table designate their particular levels of significance.

EXERCISES FOR CHAPTER 2

1. Use the Library of Congress subject heading listings to develop a list of five possible search terms for your dependent variable.
2. Find ten scholarly articles on your dependent variable.
3. Choose three scholarly articles, and for each one, identify its "what" question, dependent variable, independent variables, and conclusions.
4. Make a list of all the independent variables you find in five scholarly articles about your dependent variable.

Project Definition and Systematic Investigation

Chapters 1 and 2 described how to begin a question-based research project in international relations. Chapter 1 covered choosing and researching a topic (your dependent variable) and developing a "what" question to guide your research project. This research question guides the exploration of the cause-and-effect relationships among a set of factors (independent variables) and your dependent variable. Chapter 2 explained how to conduct a preliminary literature review in international relations. A literature review allows you to identify potentially important independent variables and to understand the conclusions reached by other scholars.

In this chapter, we'll talk about the next step, which is to set up a research roadmap—called a **research design**—to guide your specific project. A research design sets out how you will systematically organize your research process and how you will collect information and analyze it. High-quality research includes precise definitions and clear measures for observations. This chapter will explain how to set up and conduct research in this way.

There are numerous approaches to IR research. While all are question-based, there are various ways to go about finding the answer to your question. This text teaches you how to use a case-based approach to answering your research question. We chose this approach not because it is superior to other methodological forms of research, but because a case-based approach is one of the best approaches for learning conceptual and analytical skills, and because many IR scholars use this methodology. Case-based research allows you to look at the complexities of specific cases and can yield interesting findings that contribute important knowledge to the field of international relations.

A **case** is an event, issue, policy, or circumstance that you will study. A **case-based research approach** is based on the systematic gathering and comparison of evidence in one or more cases to answer a narrowly defined question. Your specific project involves choosing a framework that identifies one or more cases to incorporate into your research question. You will then trace the role of specific independent variables in explaining the outcome of your case. This approach favors precision over scope through narrowly designed projects that explore a limited number of variables in one or more cases.

This chapter describes how to:

- Choose appropriate independent variables and hypotheses
- Choose a case or cases
- Conduct research on (and measure) the variables you have chosen

Your research goal now is to answer your "what" question by using a specific case or cases to draw conclusions about the relationships among variables. Before we talk about how to proceed with these activities of case-based research, let's briefly discuss two project frameworks researchers can use within this approach.

PROJECT FRAMEWORKS

Researchers use a variety of approaches when developing their projects. Here we focus our attention on two project frameworks applicable for question-based research papers. These frameworks are meant to give you starting points for the development of analytical thinking, research, and writing in international relations.

- A **single-case–based research project** focuses on *one* case and the relationship between a dependent variable and a set of independent variables and hypotheses identified in the scholarly literature.

  Example question: What factors affected the outbreak of ethnic conflict in the former Yugoslavia in 1991–1992?
  Dependent variable: Outbreak of ethnic conflict
  Case: Yugoslavia in 1991–1992
- A **comparative-case–based research project (comparing cases)** focuses on *two or more cases* and the relationship between a single dependent variable and independent variables identified in the scholarly literature and in your own hypotheses.

  Example question: What factors affected the outbreak of ethnic conflict in the former Yugoslavia in 1991–1992 and the outbreak of ethnic conflict in Rwanda in 1994?
  Dependent variable: Outbreak of ethnic conflict
  Cases: Yugoslavia in 1991–1992 and Rwanda in 1994

Information about when to choose each framework will be discussed soon when we address how to choose cases.

CHOOSING INDEPENDENT VARIABLES AND HYPOTHESES

The first step in choosing independent variables is to go back to your notes from your review of the scholarly literature and your list of the independent variables (or factors) that scholars have found to be important to an explanation of your topic. (See Chapter 2.) This list may be very long, containing ten or more different variables. It will be very difficult to do research on all of these variables, so you will need to choose a shorter list of variables to explore in your study.

Let's use this "what" question for our example: "What factors affect the outbreak of ethnic conflict?" After conducting a review of the scholarly literature, we came up with the following list of independent variables that are thought to affect, influence, or cause the outbreak of ethnic conflict:

- A weak national government
- Border/boundary questions
- Leadership promotion of ethnic identification
- An economic downturn
- Outside political support
- Outside economic support
- Outside military support

One way to narrow the list is to come up with hypotheses or reasoned potential explanations. You can develop hypotheses in two main ways. First, you may find hypotheses discussed in the scholarly literature that you would like to test in a new case or cases. Second, you may develop hypotheses of your own based on variables you believe will most likely answer your research question. In our example, you might set out the following two hypotheses:

> H1   An increase in outside military support for opposing sides and the existence of border/boundary disputes will lead to the outbreak of ethnic conflict.
>
> H2   A leader's promotion of ethnic identification, coupled with an economic downturn, will lead to ethnic conflict.

The following independent variables are included here:

- Outside military support
- Existence of border/boundary disputes
- Leader's promotion of ethnic identification
- Economic downturn

You now can look for evidence to test whether or not your hypotheses are supported in the case(s) you choose. Also note that the hypotheses are set out in general terms. That is, you could test these hypotheses across any number of cases of ethnic conflict. And that is what political scientists try to do: they try to make general characterizations about the relationships among variables that can be applied to many cases.

CHOOSING CASES FOR RESEARCH

Once you have a question with a clear dependent variable and hypotheses that set out your tentative explanations, your project will take shape after you can choose a case or cases to study. That is, through a decision process, you can select one or more events, issues, policies, or circumstances to help you explore your research question. We know that no two situations in international relations are ever exactly alike. Therefore, you can expand the general understanding of political phenomena by exploring how independent variables affect a dependent variable in a new case or across cases. Think of cases as units of comparison for your dependent variable. If your "what" question asks about the outbreak of ethnic conflict, your cases will be examples of ethnic conflict. If your "what" question asks about a type of policy decision, your cases will be examples of such policies. Your dependent variable is your first guide to choosing a case or cases. These cases can be conflicts, crises, treaties, the actions of several decision makers, types of policies, or any other plausible comparable entity. It all depends on the question you are asking.

You should know a lot about your dependent variable already, both through general research and through your literature review. Begin with a written definition for your dependent variable, preferably found in the scholarly literature or in your textbook. If, for example, your "what" question is "What factors affect the outbreak of ethnic conflict?" you need to find a definition for ethnic conflict in your IR text. Here, again, you can rely on the work of scholars. Goldstein, for example, defines ethnic conflict as conflict

▶ WHERE TO LOOK FOR POTENTIAL CASES

Here are some sources that can help you compile a list of potential cases to use for your research project.

- Your textbook
- Scholarly literature
  - Some scholarly articles contain listings of particular groups of cases (e.g., war, conflict, crises, particular negotiations, etc.).
  - Some scholarly websites contain databases you can search.
- Websites of reputable international organizations, such as the UN, intergovernmental organizations, and nongovernmental organizations
- Websites of government agencies, such as the State Department
- Reference books, such as almanacs and books that contain useful listings (of wars, conflicts, etc.)

You can find more specific information, including particular websites and print sources, in Part II.

between "large groups of people who share ancestral, language, cultural, or religious ties and a common identity" (2003, 545). The next step is to make a list of those violent conflicts that would fall under your definition. You can use a number of sources, including almanacs, yearbooks, reference volumes, and online government resources, to help you choose cases.

After you have a list of potential cases, you will choose one or more cases (see Table 3.1). One option is to choose a **critical case** within which to test your hypotheses. A **critical case** is one that scholars suggest is historically important. If you are studying ethnic conflict, you may choose to study Rwanda because scholars have noted the scale of the violence and duration of the conflict. The most rigorous single-case analyses test hypotheses of other scholars, preferably those hypotheses that focus on different variables or theories. One example is a single-case study that tests whether realist or idealist theories offer more explanatory power.

Another option is to choose two cases across which you test your hypotheses. Here you have a number of alternatives. One is to choose cases that have similar outcomes and to test whether specific independent variables play similar roles in producing those outcomes. A second alternative involves comparisons of cases before and after an important independent variable changes. Finally, you may choose to compare cases with different outcomes to see if specific independent variables play a role in determining the outcomes. The important point to remember is that you will be comparing the same independent variables (as set out in your hypotheses) across both cases.

TABLE 3.1

Choosing Cases

Option	Purpose
Choose one case	To assess competing hypotheses from the scholarly literature, preferably those that focus on different variables or theories
Choose one case	To explore a critical case, i.e., a case that falls outside of our theoretical understanding of political phenomena or has qualities that look highly different than other similar cases
Choose two or more cases	To compare cases with similar outcomes to see if specific independent variables play similar roles
Choose two or more cases	To compare cases before and after an important independent variable changes
Choose two or more cases	To compare cases with different outcomes to see if specific independent variables play a role in determining the different outcomes

For example, suppose you are interested in explaining large-scale ethnic conflict. You may choose the former Yugoslavia and Rwanda as your cases. Both countries have experienced extremely high levels of violence. These cases allow you to compare ethnic conflicts during similar time periods but in different geographic locations. There is also a considerable amount of data available on these two conflicts. If you were interested in conflicts in Africa, you might pair Rwanda with Somalia.

Reminder: Make sure that the combination of cases and independent variables you choose differs somehow from what you found in the literature you have read. (You do not want to redo the exact same research design as someone else.) For example, it is okay if you found an article on conflict in Rwanda and Somalia, but make sure your research design adds something new by focusing on different independent variables or different hypotheses.

INFORMATION AVAILABILITY

The availability of information you will need for your research is not a trivial issue. You must have access to information to complete your project. The reliability of the results that emerge from the comparative-case analysis approach is directly related to how careful and systematic the researcher is in gathering and comparing information and data about a case or cases. Many nonindustrialized countries lack the resources to gather and publish data commonly available from wealthier countries; some societies are less open and restrict public access to some information. It is wise to select a case or cases for your project about which you'll be likely to find plenty of information. To help you find data, we include in Part II a list of sources on international relations.

This brings us to a final point about choosing cases and your research design. You must make sure that you have thought about and specified the parameters of your cases. For example, choose specific time periods as well as, in our example, specific ethnic conflicts. Suppose your "what" question is "What factors affect third-party intervention in civil wars?" You cannot possibly systematically study every intervention. You may choose to focus on one or two American interventions within a particular time period, perhaps in the post–Cold War era, or United Nations interventions in Africa during the 1990s. This narrows your question considerably and makes evidence and/or data that much easier to collect, organize, and analyze.

Once you have chosen a case or cases for your project, you have accomplished two necessary tasks. First, you have defined parameters that make your project original. Second, you have further narrowed the scope of your project to a more manageable level. Figure 3.1 presents an overview of our example research project after completing these tasks.

	General topic:	Ethnic conflict
	Research question:	What factors affect the outbreak of ethnic conflict?
	Dependent variable:	Outbreak of ethnic conflict
	Case:	Outbreak of ethnic conflict in the former Yugoslavia, 1991–1992
	Independent	Outside military support
	variables:	Existence of border/boundary disputes
		Leader's promotion of ethnic identification
		Economic downturn
	Hypotheses:	H1 An increase in outside military support for opposing sides and the existence of border/boundary disputes will lead to the outbreak of ethnic conflict.
		H2 A leader's promotion of ethnic identification, coupled with an economic downturn, will lead to ethnic conflict.

FIGURE 3.1
Research Project Overview.

DEFINING AND OPERATIONALIZING YOUR VARIABLES

You are now ready to operationalize your variables. **Operationalization** is the process used in the social sciences to define variables in terms of observable properties. Without the clear definition of terms, readers and researchers may not have a common understanding of what is being studied. The researcher is responsible for making sure that all aspects of the study are clear and replication of the study is possible.

For example, if you look at the list of variables in Figure 3.1, you might wonder what the researcher means by "outside military support." Would the presence of outside military advisors count as military support? Or does the researcher consider only the transfer of equipment and money to be outside military support? How might the researcher define a border dispute? A leader's promotion of ethnic identification? An economic downturn? You need to ask and answer these types of questions for all your variables. All operationalization decisions should be clear enough for the reader to replicate the study.

Although the operationalization of variables may seem like a fairly straightforward task, it actually involves a number of decisions that will have important consequences for the study because social scientists often measure the same variables differently. In most cases, IR researchers turn to the relevant literature for assistance in establishing definitions and measurements among cases, and we encourage you to do the same. A researcher would likely find several different definitions of military support and would use discretion in deciding which definition to adopt. Definitional decisions must be defended in the final paper, so you should choose a definition with care. We encourage you, whenever possible, to use measurements found in your textbook or in the scholarly literature. (That is one reason we suggested in Chapter 2 that you take notes on definitions while doing your literature review.)

There are several important things to keep in mind when you operationalize your variables. The first is that your measurements can be quantitative or qualitative. **Quantitative measures** involve numbers; for example, the number of dollars spent, the gross domestic product, the number of military personnel. **Qualitative measures** involve the assessment of qualities or narratives that are not quantified. Examples include the tone of a leader's speeches over time and the level of racist pronouncements. Even when using qualitative measures, you must be clear about how you arrive at your measure or assessment.

The second thing to keep in mind is that what you count and how you count it matters. Although the use of reliable data will not always yield reliable results, the use of unreliable data will always yield unreliable results. Choose your sources for data collection carefully. We recommend that you use data from library reference materials or from government sources whenever possible. Use extreme caution when acquiring data from nongovernmental sources on the Internet.

The third point we wish to make is that even if you use reliable resources for your data, you might still err if you are inconsistent and unsystematic in

◢ COMMON CONSISTENCY ERRORS

Be careful with your calculations and comparisons so you can avoid the following types of errors:

- Collecting some data in hectare measurements, some in acres
- Making some area calculations in square kilometers, others in square miles
- Comparing data based on different scales, such as deaths per 1,000 births compared with deaths per 100,000 births
- Not converting national consumption rates to per capita rates
- Using both Celsius and Fahrenheit measurements in comparisons without making conversions
- Comparing the mean average to the median average
- Not including inflation rates In comparisons of income or economic data over time

your calculations and comparisons. For instance, if you compared the gross national product of Canada and the United States but used a Canadian source for one figure and a U.S. source for the other, and then failed to convert the Canadian currency to the U.S. dollar equivalency (or vice versa), your comparison would be incorrect.

One more example will explain operationalization further. Suppose you are interested in the factors that affect whether or not a country joins a particular type of international organization. You may find in the scholarly literature that some scholars argue that a country's level of economic development will affect this. How would you measure economic development? Because the term *economic development* is discussed in a number of ways within the field and lacks a generally accepted definition among political scientists, establishing a precise definition is important. We found the following definition in an IR textbook:

> **Economic Development:** The use of land, labor and capital to produce higher standards of living, typically measured by increases in gross national product and more equitable distribution of national income. (Duncan, Jancar-Webster, and Switky 2001, 656)

This definition suggests that an adequate method for establishing a means of comparison of economic development among the cases used for this study would be to use the country's gross national product (GNP) or gross domestic product (GDP)[1] along with the country's income distribution.

Similarly, for our example about the outbreak of ethnic conflict in the former Yugoslavia, you should first begin by clearly stating how you defined the dependent variable, "outbreak in ethnic conflict." After defining the dependent variable, you could search the literature to find the best ways to define and measure the independent variables chosen for the study. Figure 3.2 shows how the complete overview might look after completing these tasks.

COLLECTING EVIDENCE

Once you have established how each variable will be defined and measured, you are ready to collect information (sometimes called evidence or data) on the particular independent variables in the case(s) you have chosen. We suggest that at this point in your project's development that you set up a physical folder (or a folder on your computer dedicated to each independent variable). The reason for this type of organizational strategy is related to the next step in the process where you will review information associated with each variable independently before looking at how variables may associate with one another. Sometimes it is difficult to know where to look for information on specific cases. We include listings for data collection in Part II.

One of the most important things to remember when you are collecting information about your independent variables is that you must put the values

---

[1]The gross domestic product of a country is the total of goods and services produced by a nation. Such information can be found in data tables in reference books available in most university libraries.

General topic:	Ethnic conflict
Research question:	What factors affect the outbreak of ethnic conflict?
Dependent variable:	Outbreak of ethnic conflict
Case:	Outbreak of ethnic conflict in the former Yugoslavia, 1991–1992
Independent variables:	Outside military support
	Existence of border/boundary disputes
	Leader's promotion of ethnic identification
	Economic downturn
Hypotheses:	H1 An increase in outside military support for opposing sides and the existence of border/boundary disputes will lead to the outbreak of ethnic conflict.
	H2 A leader's promotion of ethnic identification, coupled with an economic downturn, will lead to ethnic conflict.

Operationalization of variables:

Dependent Variable:	Outbreak of ethnic conflict
	Measurement = 1991 Public announcements by Croatia and Slovenia to secede from Yugoslavia
	Measurement = War deaths associated with formal efforts to secede
Independent Variables:	
	(IV1) Outside military support
	• Measurement 1 = dollar amount of military aid from foreign states (quantitative)
	• Measurement 2 = documented promises by foreign leaders for military support, e.g., arms, personnel, advisors (qualitative)

(IV2) Existence of border/boundary disputes	
• Measurement 1 = claims by ethnic groups to the same land, documented in speeches, interviews (qualitative)	○
• Measurement 2 = number of requests by one or more groups for mediation on border issues (quantitative)	
(IV3) Leader's promotion of ethnic identification	
• Measurement 1 = leadership statements claiming ethnic superiority, documented in major public addresses such as inaugural speeches, messages to government, major televised speeches (qualitative)	○
• Measurement 2 = leadership statements calling on one ethnic group to take a leadership role (qualitative)	
(IV4) Economic downturn	
• Level of unemployment (quantitative)	
• Level of GDP (quantitative)	
• Level of trade (quantitative)	
• Inflation rate (quantitative)	

FIGURE 3.2
Research Project Overview Including Operationalization of Variables.

in context. For example, if you find measurements for military support in 1991 (when the outbreak of ethnic conflict occurred), you must also know how this level compares to past levels. Has military support increased, or has the amount been the same for a number of years? In other words, has there been a change in the value (or assessment) of the variable?

When comparing two cases, the most common mistake students make when collecting evidence or data is that they fail to collect the same data for all their cases. For example, if a student has chosen to study the outbreak of ethnic conflict in both the former Yugoslavia, 1991–1992, and in Rwanda, 1994, he or she might gather information on military support for the first case but not the second. Sometimes this is because not all data are available for each case, but sometimes it is because students have failed to identify what they need to gather for each case.

There are a number of ways to organize your data and evidence collection. One system that works for many students is to divide a notebook into sections by variable. With each section devoted to a particular variable, create a column or row for each case. Gather the same data on each case for each variable. *Carefully organize the data you gather in a very systematic way.* Table 3.2 shows a way to organize economic data, and Table 3.3 uses this same approach to tabulate the number of speeches a leader presented to parliament during a given year (which would make it a quantitative measure).

Data have meaning only when they are viewed within a context, so you should also collect data or evidence that will allow for evaluation. For instance, if you are exploring economic effects on civil unrest, you need to know about any positive or negative changes in economic indicators. Therefore, you should collect data for more than just the year of the phenomena you are exploring. The question of how far back one needs to go is somewhat subjective. For some variables, the comparison to the prior year may be enough. For other variables, you might need to view twenty years of data. It is important, however, to remain consistent. You should strive to collect data (especially for the same variable) using

TABLE 3.2

Data on Economic Downturn

Operationalized: Level of unemployment, GDP, trade, inflation rate

Country A	Unemployment (%)	GDP (Billions of Dollars)	Trade (Total Exports, Millions of U.S. Dollars)	Inflation Rate (%)
1991	17	N/A	N/A	2.6
1992	15	N/A	N/A	5.5
1993	14	N/A	50	6.2
1994	10	1.9	75	8.3
1995	6	3.5	100	20
Country B				
1991	15	1.9	96	19.6
1992	15	1.9	94	18
1993	15	1.9	93	15
1994	13	1.9	92	10
1995	10	1.9	91	10

TABLE 3.3

Data on Leader's Promotion of Ethnic Identification

Operationalized: Major speeches incorporating ethnic rhetoric. Ethnic rhetoric includes calls for protection of the ethnic group against "enemies," calls for standing together as an ethnic group, and slogans pointing to and praising ethnic identity.

Country A	Major Speeches Calling for Protection Against Enemies	Major Speeches Calling for Standing Together as an Ethnic Group	Major Speeches Containing Slogans Praising Ethnic Identity
1991	January 5 (see notes for cite and full notes)	—	—
1992	February 8, April 30 (see notes for cite and full notes)	—	—
1993	January 15, March 16, April 5, May 12, August 21, October 21, November 15, December 2	January 15, April 5, October 21, November 15, December 2	October 21, November 15, December 2
1994	January 3, 24; February 2, 12; March 20; April 4, 9, 24; May 1, 14, 30; June 3; August 21; October 4; November 17; December 9	January 24; February 12; March 20; April 4, 9, 24; May 1, 14, 30; June 3, 23; July 22; August 4, 21; October 4; November 17, 23; December 9	May 1, 14, 30; June 3, 23; July 22; August 4, 21; October 4; November 17, 23; December 9
1995	January 16, July 21, December 17	January 16, July 21, December 17	January 2, 16; February 21; March 15; April 22; May 26; June 4; July 21; September 12; October 21; November 22; December 17
Country B			
1991	—	—	—
1992	—	—	—
1993	—	—	—
1994	—	—	—
1995	—	—	June 2

NOTES: (Keep written notes for citations and full notes, and include information here as relevant.)

the same time parameters throughout your study. For most introductory projects, we encourage students to choose either a five-year period or a ten-year period.

Note that there are ways to organize your data collection even if you are collecting qualitative data. In the example about leadership promotion of ethnic identification, you must still be consistent in defining your terms and measuring systematically. Once you have collected the information needed to measure each variable, you are ready to analyze your data and write up your project. The next chapter discusses tips for analyzing data and writing up your project in a journal article format.

FREQUENTLY ASKED QUESTIONS

"I am drowning in information. What can I do?"

- Stay focused on how you operationalized your independent variables. Gather only the information that you said you would gather.
- You may need to limit your study to a smaller time period.
- You may need to change how you operationalize a variable. For instance, if you are looking at newspaper coverage, you may wish to limit your search to only front-page articles or articles that appear on one or two days of the week.

"I cannot find enough information on my variables. What should I do?"

- Go back to the articles you used in your literature review, and look for where they obtained some of their information.
- Reexamine how you operationalized your variables. Explore other ways to do so.

"I need data but cannot find a source. Where can I find some data?"

- Use Part II of this book for suggestions.
- Use the footnotes and citations of articles and books on your topic to locate where other authors have gotten data.
- Ask your research librarian for guidance in finding electronic and hard copy data sources.
- Explore government websites for data sets.
- A number of nongovernmental organizations (NGOs) gather data in conjunction with governments and institutions that oversee international treaties. Identify treaty websites, and look for data sets and lists of NGOs that are assisting in data collection. Then go to the websites of these NGOs. *Note*: We always advise students to ask their course professors for approval before using any nongovernmental or nonacademic Internet sources of data (i.e., those whose website addresses don't end in either .gov or .edu).

EXERCISES FOR CHAPTER 3

1. Develop two hypotheses that incorporate four independent variables for your research question.
2. Develop a list of potential cases for a chosen (or assigned) "what" research question. Make sure that you cite your sources.
3. Choose two cases for your chosen (or assigned) research question, and explain the reasons that you chose these two.
4. Conduct general research, and write up the story of the two cases.
5. Write up a research design like the one shown in Figure 3.2.
6. Develop a grid to organize data collection for your independent variables.

Analysis and Writing

Researchers generally do not begin the writing process for their research projects until they have gathered all of the information necessary to respond to their research questions. That means that their writing begins after about 80 percent of their research project is completed. Writing the final paper is just one step of a complex research process that first involves developing an original research question; conducting a thorough literature review; creating a research design that identifies independent variables, hypotheses, and cases; and gathering evidence in a systematic way. If you have taken good notes as you worked your way through the research process and carefully operationalized your variables for evidence collection, you will be prepared to write a paper that brings all of these different phases together.

After following the steps outlined earlier in this text, what is left to complete your project is to analyze the information you have gathered and write up your findings in a final paper. This sounds easy, but for most of us writing is difficult. Moving from thoughts to written words often requires several drafts before a paper is ready for review by others. This is true for students and professors alike. Writing clearly and concisely takes patience, and in most cases professional researchers are under the constraints of guidelines issued by publishers that require specific formats and page limitations for any paper submission. Students face similar constraints, including those related to page length, specific citation formats, and structure.[2] This chapter will help prepare you to write your research paper in a clear and organized way.

AN OVERVIEW OF THE WRITING PROCESS

It is best to obtain specific instructions from your professor before beginning to write because there are numerous approaches used to document research. In this book we describe how to document an international relations research project in a format typically found in IR journals. This format includes seven written sections of varying length that together form a paper approximately

---

[2]This text does not extensively cover style issues such as word usage, sentence structure, or punctuation.

twenty to twenty-five pages long. You will likely find this length necessary to fully describe your research project and its findings. Later in this chapter we provide more detail about what type of information should be included in each of the seven sections; for now, here is a brief description of the sections in the order that they will appear in your paper.

- **Abstract:** Begin your paper with a one-paragraph synopsis of your project that includes your research question, the importance of studying this question, the variables you addressed in the study, and the conclusions reached from the evidence you collected. (Approximate length: one-quarter page.)
- **Introduction:** The introduction provides general information about the topic, including a brief history. Your introduction may also include an overview of how your paper structurally unfolds. (Approximate length: two to three pages.)
- **Literature review:** This section describes the scholarly literature and should explain (at the end) how your research question fits within this literature. We suggest clearly stating your research question at the end of this section and introducing it again in the next. (Approximate length: three to five pages.)
- **Research design (methodology):** This section describes the project format, including your choice of cases, the description and operationalization of the dependent and independent variables, and your choice of sources and analytical methods. (Approximate length: three to six pages.)
- **Case presentation, analysis, and discussion of findings:** This section is the heart of the paper. A presentation of the case(s) sets out the variables and the context. This is followed by a discussion of the evidence, the strength of relationships, and a response to the research question. (Approximate length: ten to twelve pages.)
- **Conclusion:** Regardless of whether your hypotheses were supported by your research, the conclusion section is an opportunity to discuss the importance of your findings. One suggestion for writing your conclusion is to link your findings back to what other similar studies have found. You might also discuss problems you encountered finding information and other factors that may account for your findings. This section should also contain a brief discussion of the project's limitations and what type of studies would further enhance our understanding of the topic. (Approximate length: one page.)
- **Bibliography or reference list:** This section contains the sources you used, set out in alphabetical order by author's last name and in an acceptable style or format. The bibliography or reference list is important because it shows your readers where you got your information. (Approximate length: varies, depending on the number of sources you used, which may be based on what your professor requires.)

Perhaps the most important point to remember as you begin the writing and analysis phase of your project is that no matter how hard you have worked or how extensively you have researched your project, if you fail to communicate your findings clearly or present your project professionally, all of your hard work will go unrewarded. Students disappointed with grades lower than they expected sometimes comment that they believe substance should count far more than form. Although we agree that this is a valid argument, the reader of your paper must believe that you have seriously approached your research. Important research sloppily presented—full of typographical errors, spelling problems, imperfect citations, and careless sentence structure—undermines the credibility of the research. *Style* is important.[3] Because it is often difficult to identify one's own writing mistakes, we suggest that you have someone else proofread your manuscript for errors before submission.

A second important point is that the project paper seldom represents all of the research the author completed during the course of the project. When writing a question-based research paper, you will inevitably make choices about what to include and what not to include. Data gathered early in the project's research phases may have no utility at the completion of the project. Before you finalized your project's research question, you may have read some scholarly literature that no longer applies at all. Include in your paper only the information that directly relates to your research question.

Another challenge associated with writing research papers is that you must describe complex political phenomena as succinctly as possible. The difficulty emerges not from a lack of knowledge of a topic but from overfamiliarity. You may find that several of your descriptions sound perfectly clear to you, but to someone else the manuscript may lack the level of description necessary to follow your thoughts. The only way to know if you have clearly articulated your thoughts is to have an outside reader provide feedback on the clarity of your paper.

One of the biggest mistakes you can make is to overstate your findings. You must learn to be humble about your project findings. Political scientists never "prove" anything. We may find "support" for our conclusions or "evidence to suggest," but no matter how many times we observe the same phenomena, politics takes place in a world of countless variables. No two situations are ever exactly alike. We may observe enough similarities among related events to form theories and reliable assumptions about different situations, but we also know that there will almost always be exceptions to general trends, practices, and activities.

When writing your paper, remember that you are exploring a research question using a single case or a very limited number of cases. You cannot be sure that your findings will hold in other similar circumstances. The key is to link your findings back to the scholarly literature. You should note that your findings either support or do not support what other scholars have found, but do not overstate your findings by indicating that your research proves something or that all other research conclusions are wrong because you found a case that does not fit with what scholars understand about other similar cases. We actually expect that there will be situations that do not fit with what generally occurs. Finding an exception is interesting and important to our understanding of political

---

[3]Although this text focuses on the research process and not on style, you'll find some helpful style tips and resources in Part III.

phenomena. For example, if a researcher finds that one treaty failed when all similar other treaties did not, this does not mean that the factors that scholars have identified as generally leading to treaty compliance are incorrect. The writing of scholars often reflects this type of exception through the use of language such as "in most cases," "in general," "with limited exceptions," and so on.

Another form of overstatement comes from the use of language that suggests more than can reasonably be claimed. You should avoid using words such as "extremely," "extraordinarily," "highly," "never," and "always" when describing your findings. After all, you can only reliably draw conclusions about the cases used in your study, not about the entire universe of possible cases. It is also unlikely, given your time and resource constraints, that you explored all possible variables for your cases.

When writing up research, it is better to understate your findings than overstate them. In the end, your research project is not designed to function as a persuasive tool. You entered the project as an open-minded researcher, and you should continue that perspective until the project is completed. With these points in mind, we now turn to more detailed descriptions and instructions for how to transform your project into a high-quality research paper.

WRITING EACH SECTION OF YOUR RESEARCH PAPER

Anyone who has ever written a paper has struggled at one time or another with getting the first sentence on paper. This agonizing step is often easier with a research paper than with a persuasive paper or critique because the research paper does not have to be written in a specific order. You are not building an argument; you are documenting a research project and its findings. In fact, it is often easier and more logical to write the middle of your paper first.

If you are writing your paper in a journal article format, as we mentioned earlier, your paper should have seven sections:

- abstract
- introduction
- literature review
- research design (methodology)
- case presentation, analysis, and discussion of findings
- conclusion
- bibliography or reference list

We suggest that you write the abstract and the conclusion last, but you may choose to write any of the other sections first. However, you should construct a good outline for each section before you begin writing so that you have a roadmap that will keep you on the right path if you are writing in a different order. In the following subsections, we provide general tips for each section to help you pull together the appropriate information for your paper. Just remember that even though we describe the sections in the order they will appear in your paper, you do not need to write your paper in this order.

THE ABSTRACT

The abstract is a short but very important part of your paper. The abstract should be no longer than a paragraph, succinctly stating what the project was about, the political context of the study, and the most significant findings or conclusion of the study. The order in which you introduce each of these components, however, is within your discretion. Here is a suggested outline for an abstract.

A. **Basis and structure of the study:** Transform your research question into a project statement.

B. **"So what" response:** Briefly describe the relationship of this study to other IR literature.

C. **Methodology:** Tell the reader what case(s) you used for your study and your method of analysis. If you are using the methodology described in this text, you would indicate in your abstract that you used a single-case analysis or a comparative-case approach for your method of study. Be sure to tell the reader which case(s) you explored in your study, but leave the details for later in your paper.

D. **Most significant finding(s):** Summarize the most important finding(s) from your study in no more than one or two sentences.

In figure 4.1, we have placed letters that correspond to this outline so you can see how the authors built each component into their paper's abstract.

Abstract

[A]This study examines the relationship between national corporate tax policies and globalization. [A]Specifically, we empirically focus on whether the internationalization of markets has led to lower corporate taxes across OECD countries. [B]In contrast to other studies, we consider whether government education and research programs provide policy makers additional capacity to deal with the pressures of globalization. [B]Such government programs may enhance tax policy independence in an era of globalization. [B]Additionally, we consider whether the interaction of government education and research programs with global capital flows permits governments to modify the demand to lower corporate taxes. [C]Using Ordinary Least Square analysis on a cross-sectional time series data set comprised of 17 OECD countries for the years 1982–1991, [D]we find evidence of an association between government education and higher corporate taxes. [D]Moreover, we demonstrate that the interaction between education policies and capital flow dampens the need for national governments to lower corporate taxes.

FIGURE 4.1

Example of an abstract. Superscript letters indicate elements from the outline described in this chapter. (Source of abstract: Gelleny and McCoy 2001, 509.)

THE INTRODUCTION

The introduction presents the topic of your paper. In this section you should include enough *general* information to draw readers into the project and provide a context sufficient for them to understand your research goal. Think of your introduction as the setup for your paper. An effective way to organize an introduction is to first discuss the dependent variable associated with your research project (as stated without the case details), then briefly discuss your case(s), and finally end your introduction by clearly stating your specific research question.

For example, suppose your research question is "What domestic factors best explain the United States' decisions to use military intervention in Somalia's internal conflict in 1992 but not in Rwanda's in 1994?" The dependent variable is U.S. military interventions, and your case selections are Somalia and Rwanda. If you intend to have a brief introduction, you obviously cannot discuss every U.S. military intervention that has ever taken place. You will need to choose a time frame that provides a reasonable context for your specific study. You might limit the discussion to a brief rundown of military interventions during the last twenty-five years or those that occurred in the post–Cold War era. Or you might choose to discuss only U.S. interventions related to ethnic conflicts. Just remember that the general discussion of your dependent variable should establish the context for why the exploration of your research question is both interesting and valuable.

Follow your discussion of the dependent variable with a brief discussion of your case selection. Entice the reader into reading your paper by stating what is interesting about the case or cases you chose to explore, as opposed to other cases you could have selected. Limit your discussion, however, to brief comments, and expand on them in your paper's methodology section. If you were using our example research question, you would likely provide a brief summary of what is *obviously* similar and different about Rwanda and Somalia. You would want to make sure the reader knows that the United States intervened in one case but not the other. The following information would be appropriate in your introduction:

- the location of each country
- the beginning of each conflict
- the duration of each conflict
- the timing of U.S. interventions
- references to other countries that intervened
- the human toll related to the conflicts (deaths, refugees, migration)

After you have introduced both the dependent variable and your case selection, you should then conclude your introduction by clearly stating your research question in the form of a statement rather than a question. In our example, you could end your introduction by stating, "This study explores which domestic factors best explain the United States' decisions to use military intervention in Somalia's internal conflict in 1992 but not in Rwanda's in 1994."

THE LITERATURE REVIEW

As we discussed earlier in this text, a defining feature of IR research is a study's connection to other research in the field. The literature review section provides this link. The literature review describes the findings of other researchers who have written on subjects related to your project. Included are studies broadly associated with your dependent variable and highly similar to your study. You should not write the literature review section as if you were writing a story because developing a chronology is not the purpose of including a discussion of the scholarly literature. The literature review should describe the research of others and highlight the important independent variables, theories, and conclusions of scholars in the field.

Not all of the literature you reviewed earlier in the research process may be appropriate for inclusion in your literature review. You will need to sort through your notes and decide what to discuss. Scholars tend to vary in how much literature they choose to discuss in their research papers. Some research journals encourage significant discussion of the scholarly literature; others strictly constrain literature discussions by establishing very tight page constraints. We mention this because one professor may give you considerable flexibility in how many pages you may use to write your literature review, while another may ask you to be fairly concise in your literature discussion. Whichever is the case, keep in mind that the easiest way to organize a literature review is to start with a discussion of the research that is broadly or generally related to your project and then gradually work your way toward discussing research that is most closely and specifically related. If you are under tight page constraints, include only the literature most closely related to your project. If you have plenty of latitude, you may broaden your literature review to include articles that are generally but not closely related to your specific study.

Organization of the Literature Review

In Chapter 2 we suggested that you collect the information from each scholarly resource on a single piece of paper or a note card. Begin organizing your scholarly literature research by grouping similar works. We suggest that you resist trying to organize these studies in your head and instead place your note sheets or note cards with the individual study information into physical groupings of similar studies. Try to categorize the studies as best you can in terms of how they relate in similarity to the dependent variable of your study. For instance, if you were using our example research question, "What domestic factors best explain the United States' decisions to use military intervention in Somalia's internal conflict in 1992 but not in Rwanda's in 1994?" you may have found research studies that discuss factors that **precipitate external intervention in internal conflicts by bordering states.** You may have found studies that explore factors that **precipitate intervention by hegemonic states.** You may have also found studies specifically about **outside interventions into the internal affairs of African states.** All of these are related to the same dependent variable of international intervention but they represent sub-topics of this dependent variable. Before you begin writing, systematically group the articles you have read according to these sub-topics. Then, rather than discuss each article individually, discuss the articles by grouping.

Studies most closely related to your dependent variable are generally discussed last with those more generally associated discussed first. Therefore, with our example, the group of studies on border state interventions would be discussed first because this group of studies would be only generally related to our dependent variable. The group of studies associated with U.S. interventions in Africa would be discussed last because these studies are closely related to the dependent variable of U.S. intervention into Somalia. Figure 4.2 is an illustration of what we mean to physically group your articles and then order the groups for discussion in your literature review.

Content of the Lierature Review

If you have unlimited pages available for writing your literature review, include a summary of all of the article groupings. If your professor limits the number of pages you may use for your literature review and it is necessary to condense your research, drop the most broadly related articles from your discussion and discuss only those that are closely related to your dependent variable.

The most important thing for you to remember is that *you should not individually summarize every article that you include in your literature review.* Rather, you should synthesize the findings of the research. *Write summaries of each group* of studies. Note that it is highly likely that some articles will be discussed more than once in your literature review because they will contain information related to different categories(this means that you may develop

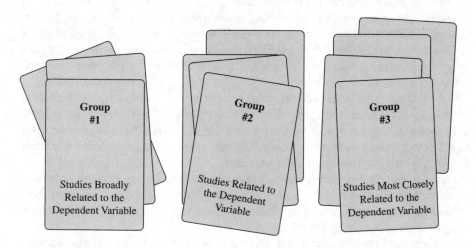

FIGURE 4.2
Organizing the Literature Review.

Group your summaries, then discuss summaries by grouping. Note, you may use more than three groups.

groupings more than once with articles falling into more than one grouping). For instance, large-scale research projects sometimes provide broad findings in addition to specific findings. In such a case, you might reference the study twice: once when talking about broad results and once when addressing more specifically related research findings.

When you begin writing your literature review there is no need for a long introduction to this section of your paper. Your paper's introduction will serve as the lead in to the literature review. You should simply jump into this section of your paper by stating how the scholarly research on your dependent variable is organized. This would roughly be a summary of your initial study groupings. Then start discussing your first group of articles. Discussion points could include:

- Which articles reach the same conclusion but use a slightly different case or methodology to arrive at that conclusion?
- Which articles were about long-term studies?
- Which are studies of isolated events?
- Which studies had similar results?
- Which studies had contradictory findings?

Important for this type of introductory paper, after completing your discussion of the major scholarly literature groupings, you should devote a section of your literature review to discussing the independent variables you used incorporated into your specific project. Because your study uses a limited number of independent variables and cases, it is extremely important that your literature review contain a clear discussion of each of these chosen variables. In fact, if you must limit your literature review to only a short section in your paper, focus on the discussion of your independent variables. If you have chosen to test the hypotheses of other scholars, make sure you discuss these in the literature review as well. This will link your findings to other scholarly research. We suggest that you conclude this section of your paper with a sentence or two about your study and then end with your research question.

As you can imagine, the literature review is the most highly cited section of your paper because it specifically talks about the research of others. Whether you use footnotes for your references or parenthetical citations is a matter of personal preference (yours or your professor's). Your citations must be accurate and follow a consistent format.

In figure 4.3, we provide an abbreviated student literature review from a research paper on the factors that affect U.S. intervention in humanitarian crises. Look at how the author discusses the scholarly literature. Note how studies were grouped and synthesized.

Writing a literature review is often a new skill for students, and as with any skill, you need to practice it. Since you have read a number of scholarly journal articles, you have read a number of literature reviews. Almost all journal articles contain them. As you read more journal articles and write more literature reviews, your skills will improve.

Literature Review
Erin McFee
What factors affect U.S. intervention in humanitarian crises?
Cases: Democratic Republic of Congo and Sudan

Gross violations of human rights, mass displacements of popula-
tions, genocide, and state failure are common occurrences in today's
world. Many of these humanitarian crises are the result of intrastate
conflicts in third-world countries and are particularly prevalent on the
African continent. This has resulted not only in literature seeking to explain this phenomenon (Henderson and Singer 2000) but also in a wide
range of literature on interventions by outside forces in these conflicts.
The response to the development of increasing occurrences of intrastate
conflict resulting in humanitarian crises has been calls for increased international intervention. This has led to a reevaluation of international
norms such as sovereignty and security (Dowty and Loescher 1996) and
a plethora of literature on international law concerning intervention
and justification of interventions (Dowty and Loescher 1996; Fixal and
Smith 1998; Weil 2001). This literature suggests an increase in the ac-
ceptance and legitimacy of humanitarian armed interventions despite
the contradictions that often arise in regard to principles such as sovereignty. Some scholars have addressed the conditions that most often
lead to successful interventions (Carment and Rowlands 1998; Krain
2005; Regan 2002). Other scholars have studied the effect of intervention on the duration of conflict (Regan 2002, 1996; Blach-Lindsay
and Enterline 2000; Krain 2005).

In comparison to literature on legality and justification, relatively few
scholars have looked at why nations or institutions choose to intervene
(Jakobsen 1996; Werner 2000; Lowenheim 2003; Regan 1998). Factors
noted here include the saliency of a country defined by location, resources, and former political relationships. Other factors include the
likelihood of success (Jakobsen 1996; Regan 1998), the ramifications
of civil war and the movement of refugees for international stability
(Forman 1972; Dowty and Loescher 1996; Werner 2000; Yoon 1997; Regan
1998), and public opinion (Klarevas 2000; Burk 1999; Boettcher 2004;
Yoon 1997; Regan 1998; Nincic 1997).

Very few scholars have taken into account moral accountability and
prestige as a factor that affects a country's decision to intervene in an
intrastate conflict. Lowenheim (2003), however, finds evidence that it
could be a substantial contributing factor in some cases. Regan (1998)

claims humanitarian issues do matter in decisions to respond to conflicts; however, it is not clear if action is based on a genuine feeling of responsibility or a calculated decision to bolster image. This paper will examine this factor, along with saliency, the likelihood of success, degree of instability, and public opinion in the cases of the Democratic Republic of Congo and Sudan.

[The following reference list would appear at the end of the paper in the references section.]

Blach-Lindsay, Dylan, and Andrew Enterline. 2000. Killing time: The world politics of civil war duration, 1820–1992. *International Studies Quarterly* 44:615–42.

Boettcher, William A. 2004. Military intervention decisions regarding humanitarian crises. *Journal of Conflict Resolution* 48, no. 3:331–55.

Burk, James. 1999. Public support for peacekeeping in Lebanon and Somalia: Assessing the casualties hypothesis. *Political Science Quarterly* 114, no. 1:53–78.

Carment, David, and Dane Rowlands. 1998. Three's company: Evaluating third-party intervention in intrastate conflict. *Journal of Conflict Resolution* 42, no. 5:572–99.

Carola. 2001. The protection-neutrality dilemma in humanitarian emergencies: Why the need for military intervention? *International Migration Review* 35, no. 1:79–116.

Dowty, Alan, and Gil Loescher. 1996. Refugee flows as grounds for international action. *International Security* 21, no. 1:43–71.

Fixal, Mona, and Dan Smith. 1998. Humanitarian intervention and just war. *Mershon International Studies Review* 42, no. 2:283–312.

Forman, Eric M. 1972. Civil wars as a source of international violence. *The Journal of Politics* 34, no. 4:1111–34.

Henderson, Errol, and David Singer. 2000. Civil war in the post-colonial world, 1946–92. *Journal of Peace Research* 37, no. 3:275–99.

Jakobsen, Peter. 1996. National interest, humanitarianism or CNN: What triggers UN peace enforcement after the Cold War? *Journal of Peace Research* 33, no. 2:205–15.

Klarevas, Louis. 2000. Trends: The United States peace operation in Somalia. *The Public Opinion Quarterly* 64, no. 4:523–40.

Krain, Matthew. 2005. International intervention and the severity of genocides and politicides. *International Studies Quarterly* 49, no. 3:363–87.

Lowenheim, Oded. 2003. Do ourselves credit and render a lasting service to mankind: British oral prestige, humanitarian intervention, and the Barbary pirates. *International Studies Quarterly* 47:23–48.

Nincic, Miroslav. 1997. Loss aversion and the domestic context of military intervention. *Political Research Quarterly* 50, no. 1:97–120.

Regan, Patrick M. 1996. Conditions of successful third-party intervention in intrastate conflicts. *The Journal of Conflict Resolution* 40, no. 2 (June): 336–59.

———. 1998. Choosing to intervene: Outside interventions in internal conflicts. *The Journal of Politics* 60, no. 3:754–79.

———. 2002. Third-party interventions and the duration of intrastate conflict. *The Journal of Conflict Resolution* 46, no. 1:55–73.

Werner, Suzanne. 2000. Deterring intervention: The stakes of war and third-party involvement. *American Journal of Political Science* 44, no. 4:720–32.

Yoon, Mi Yung. 1997. Explaining U.S. intervention in third-world internal wars, 1945–1989. *Journal of Conflict Resolution* 41, no. 4:580–602.

FIGURE 4.3

Example of a student literature review and the related reference list entries. (Source of excerpts: McFee 2007.)

COMMON ERRORS IN WRITING A LITERATURE REVIEW

Students may make a number of common mistakes when first learning how to write a literature review:

- introducing studies but not discussing their findings
- using information from scholarly resources to write a narrative about the topic rather than describing the studies themselves
- discussing one study after another without discussing how they are linked to one another
- failing to state common findings among a group of studies
- not carefully identifying independent variables explored in each study, which then makes comparison and generalization about how articles are related very difficult
- including articles that have only slight or no connection to the research study

If you take care to avoid these errors, you will make your research paper much stronger.

THE RESEARCH DESIGN (METHODOLOGY)

The methodology section of a research paper is written differently than any other section. It is meant to be a technical discussion developed for the purpose of peer review and replication. Your methodology section should include (1) choice of cases, (2) your hypotheses along with justification for them, and (3) detailed discussion of how variables were measured and compared (including definitions and scales used in your analysis and the sources of your data or information). If you are an advanced student using more sophisticated data analysis techniques than simple frequency comparisons, you should also discuss the methodological tool(s) used in your analysis.

Discussion of Cases

We suggest that your methodology section begin with a restatement of your research question in the first paragraph. While this may be redundant if you also included your research question at the end of your literature review, after reintroducing your research question, inform the reader what case or cases you chose for your study. You should write up this section describing the method you used for case selection (as described in Chapter 3). For example, if you chose particular cases of conflict to explore because they had the most battle deaths on the African continent since WWII, then you should say this is why you chose these cases rather than those with lower battle deaths. If you chose to look at two particular treaties because they had high rates of signatures parties but low rates of ratification, you should explain this and why this makes these cases important for exploration. Make it clear to the reader that while your choice of cases was to some degree subjective, selection was not arbitrary.

Discussing Hypotheses

Another reason for reintroducing your research question at the beginning of your Analysis section of your paper is that your question provides a quick setup for discussion of your hypotheses. As we also indicated in Chapter 3, the difference between simply guessing and formulating a hypothesis is that when forming a hypothesis, the researcher uses established knowledge to speculate on the relationship between variables. When discussing the development of hypotheses for your study, we suggested that you formulate hypotheses using variables discussed by other researchers rather than trying to divine them autonomously. If you used this method, you will need to clearly state not only your hypotheses but also the basis you used to formulate them, taking care to cite the authors you looked to in order to formulate these hypotheses.

Note: Even though you will likely formulate your hypotheses based on your specific case project, you should state your hypotheses in a general form so that they could be tested in other cases as well. Hence, you should not refer to your specific case(s) when stating your hypotheses.

For example, let's take this research question: "What factors explain the United States' support of the Montreal Protocol for the elimination of chlorofluorocarbons but not the Kyoto Protocol to limit greenhouse gas emissions?" The study's hypotheses may include the following:

H1   United States ratification of international environmental agreements will not occur if domestic interest group opposition is strong and public opinion is unfavorable.

H2   Partisan control of Congress is not a deciding factor in the ratification of international environmental agreements if there is strong public support and international cooperation on the issue.

As you discuss the first hypothesis, be sure to mention which scholars (from your literature review) suggest that domestic interest group opposition may affect whether or not international agreements are ratified. Do the same for public opinion. Then give a brief explanation of why it would make sense to you (and the readers) that if domestic interest group opposition is strong and public opinion is unfavorable, the United States would not ratify an international environmental agreement. This may be as simple as stating that in the American political system, interest groups and public opinion have a significant effect on the behavior of the Senate, which ratifies agreements.

When discussing the second hypothesis, set out which scholars suggest that a particular party's control of Congress (partisan control) will or won't be important for an explanation of why an international agreement is ratified. Do the same for the presence of international cooperation. You have already mentioned those who have studied public opinion when discussing the first hypothesis, so you do not necessarily have to repeat that information. Then explain why it would be plausible that partisan control will not significantly affect whether or not an agreement is ratified if there is public and international support. The idea in this section is to explain how your hypotheses were developed and why they make sense or are plausible.

Discussing Measurement and Sources of Data or Information

Once you have introduced your hypotheses, you need to explain the method of comparison or measurement you used to test each hypothesis—but you should leave the discussion of findings for the analysis section of your paper. This includes measurements for each variable. Again, there is no set style for doing this, but the goal must be to describe the methodology clearly enough that the study can be replicated. Some researchers write out their methodology in paragraph form, while others use bullets, tables, and charts to explain their methods. You should consult your course professor for her or his preference on style. We generally suggest using a paragraph format if your variables are fairly simple and easy to describe. If your variables require several measurements or the use of scales in order to compare the variables over time, we suggest that you use other organizational formats. In addition, you must include the sources for your data or information. If you are measuring public opinion, for example, where did you get the numbers you use in your research? Remember that in this section you do not tell us what the numbers are; you tell us what you have measured (e.g., public opinion) and where you got the numbers that you present in the case study and analysis section that follows your discussion of the research design. Figures 4.4 and 4.5 provide simple examples for how to approach writing a methodology. Note that in these examples, one can see where the author provides definitions for terms, descriptions for how variables are measured, and the rationale for methodological choices.

This study's dependent variable is the United States' support of the Montreal Protocol and the Kyoto Protocol. For purposes of this study, we define support as formal Senate ratification of the protocol by the United States Congress. We chose to measure support in this manner, as opposed to considering the United States' initial agreement to the protocol, because such protocols are not binding for the United States unless ratified by the United States Congress. Therefore, . . .

FIGURE 4.4
Example of a methodology section: operationalizing the dependent variable.

This study explores four independent variables: (1) public support for ratification of each protocol, (2) domestic interest group opposition, (3) partisan control of the executive and legislative branches of government following negotiations, and (4) level of international cooperation for each protocol.

Public support was measured by using public opinion polls published by The Gallup Poll during the year following when the United States became a signature party to each protocol. We categorized public opinion in three categories: low, moderate, and strong support. Public support of 30 percent or less was categorized as low public support. Public support of 31–60 percent was considered moderate. Public support of 61–100 percent was considered to be strong.

Domestic interest group opposition was defined as those groups that contributed oral testimony before the congressional committees that conducted hearings on the protocols and those interest groups that submitted written statements to Congress regarding the protocols. Sources for this information included the Congressional Record and transcripts of congressional committee hearing records obtained through http://thomas.loc.gov. . . .

FIGURE 4.5
Example of a methodology section: operationalizing the independent variables.

THE CASE PRESENTATION, ANALYSIS, AND DISCUSSION OF FINDINGS

Before beginning any analysis, there are a few things to remember as you move forward with your analysis.

First, using a narrow range of variables and only a few cases makes it difficult to confidently generalize about your findings. A case study methodology allows you to observe which variables are *likely* to have had an effect on the dependent variable, but you will not be able to discern which variable *may have* been more important than another. However, uncertainty is acceptable if the researcher uses analytical skills to make reasonable assessments of which variables may have been important.

Second is to note that we keep using phrasing such as "likely" and "may have." That is because when analyzing data and evidence, a researcher has no way to know with certainty which variables may have been most important in explaining a dependent variable unless the researcher is absolutely sure that he or she looked at all possible independent variables. (In your research project, you will address only a limited number.) In most cases, political scientists look at a range of variables but seldom all possible variables. Political scientists must therefore recognize that their analysis is merely the best assessment among the variables they chose. That means being humble in both one's assessments and one's presentation of results. If you have been careful in how you have gathered information and systematic in how you analyze this information, you can draw interesting and valid conclusions. To some degree, however, the strength of your arguments will hinge on how well you lay out your study's findings. In this sense, you must translate the evidence into a format that is understandable and if you are using more than one case, evidence that can be compared across cases.

While there is no set order formula for how best to write up your analysis, one approach is to use the following sequence in your paper.

If using only one case:

1. Provide a general description of the case
2. Layout the evidence for the first variable
3. Analyze the evidence for the first variable
4. Layout the evidence for the second variable
5. Analyze the evidence for the second variable
6. Continue this sequence until you have covered all of your variables
7. Discuss the variables in the context of the hypotheses
8. Develop conclusions

If using more than one case:

9. Provide a general description of the cases
10. Layout the evidence for the first variable for case one and then for case two
11. Analyze the evidence for the first variable as it applies to case one and then as it applies to case two
12. Layout the evidence for the second variable for case one and then for case two

13. Analyze the evidence for the second variable as it applies to case one and then as it applies to case two
14. Continue this sequence until you have covered all of your variables
15. Discuss the variables within the context of the hypotheses

Analyzing Data

In Chapter 3 we suggested that you create a folder for each variable in your study and then use that folder for the collection of information and evidence associated with that variable. We suggested this because your task in the analysis section of your paper is to distill down all of the information and evidence you have collected on each of the variables in your study, into summary form that can be used to respond to your hypotheses and ultimately to answer your research question. Your first task then, is to figure out how best to present the data or evidence. Your second task is to interpret the data or evidence.

Keep in mind, you may have a folder that is overflowing with information. Your task as a researcher and scholar is to process this information for the reader. Often a graph, chart, figure or table may explain a variable better than written description. Table 4.1 shows a hypothetical comparison of unemployment data from two countries. You can see how this table conveys a lot of information about this variable (unemployment) over a long period of time for two countries in a very succinct manner. (Note: If this table was included in a research paper, the table would need to include a source for where the data were obtained). If you use a graphic of this sort, you should also resist giving a detailed description. When using graphs, charts, figures, and other illustrations to convey information about variables, keep your discussion of the variables to issues that need additional clarification or highlighting.

TABLE 4.1

Analyzing the Strength of Independent Variables

Research question: What factors contributed to the onset of ethnic conflict in countries A and B in 1994?
Dependent variable: Onset of ethnic conflict in country A and country B in 1994
Independent variable 1 (IV1): Unemployment

IV1, Case 1 (Country A)	IV1, Case 2 (Country B)
1984: 20% unemployment	1984: 6% unemployment
1986: 21% unemployment	1986: 4% unemployment
1988: 19% unemployment	1988: 8% unemployment
1990: 20% unemployment	1990: 6% unemployment
1992: 22% unemployment	1992: 14% unemployment
1994: 20% unemployment	1994: 20% unemployment

Analysis of variables should entail looking at how the data have changed over time and patterns of activity. If you are using more than one case, analyze the data from a single variable for each individual case before comparing the data across cases. Finally, we suggest that you reflect on your hypotheses after you have analyzed the independent variable data. In table 4.1 we illustrate two different scenarios one might find when collecting data on unemployment levels.

In both cases unemployment was at 20 percent at the onset of ethnic conflict in 1994. What assumptions can be made about the data? By U.S. standards, both countries had high unemployment rates. So can we assume that unemployment may have been a factor in both cases? To make any assumptions about whether or not the high rates of unemployment contributed to the onset of ethnic conflict, we need to establish a context for understanding the data. Certainly, a 20 percent unemployment rate in the United States would be both rare and economically destabilizing since unemployment rates in this country have seldom exceeded double digits since the Great Depression. But unemployment in many countries around the world has exceeded this level for decades. In some cases this has been highly destabilizing, and in other cases countries have adapted to such levels. Therefore, we need to rely on comparison data so that we have some sense of whether the unemployment rates of either country were atypical for those cases. This shows how important context is to your analysis.

In the first case, unemployment remained relatively stable at the high rate of approximately 20 percent for a decade. Continued high unemployment may have contributed to destabilization in country A, but one cannot assume with any certainty that this level alone was responsible for the onset of conflict; otherwise, why did it not occur the previous year or even three years earlier? In country A, it would be safer to assume that unemployment coupled with other variables may better explain the onset of the conflict. In the second example in table 4.1, you can see that unemployment levels more than doubled in the four years prior to the onset of the conflict after being relatively stable for more than half a decade. It would be reasonable to assume that the rapid increase in unemployment levels in country B contributed to destabilization and conflict more so than the high steady rate of unemployment noted in country A.

If you developed a single-case–based project, each variable should be explained in your final paper in much the same way as the thought process you used when analyzing and drawing conclusions about individual variables. If you developed a comparative-case–based project, you should discuss in your paper each variable as it applies to each country first, then compare the variables to one another. It is likely that by the time you have looked at each individual variable, you may have reached some conclusion about what factors may best explain your dependent variable, or you may have reached the conclusion that none of the variables explain it. You should resist discussing these conclusions, however, until you have discussed your hypotheses. Only after you have discussed each individual variable should you discuss your hypotheses.

Discussing Hypotheses

When a researcher develops hypotheses, he or she is making educated guesses. But until data are gathered and careful observation is made, they remain guesses. Therefore, even though hypotheses were based on the best available information (such as the results from other studies), political phenomena are not static. No two cases are exactly alike, and even the most carefully considered hypotheses can be wrong. Reaching the conclusion that your hypotheses were not correct is fine as long as you were careful and systematic in gathering your data or evidence to explore them. If after looking at your data you find that your hypotheses were incorrect, you should not go back and change them so that they reflect your conclusions. It is okay to refute a hypothesis in your case. In fact, sometimes, finding the unexpected is far more interesting than finding the expected.

Because we encouraged you to combine more than one variable in your initial hypotheses, it may not be easy in all cases to deduce whether or not your hypotheses are supported by the data. Without multiple cases for comparison, your analysis will be preliminary. You can discuss only what you see, and you should not try to extrapolate beyond what you found. Therefore, you need to carefully explain the reasoning you used to draw your conclusions about your initial hypotheses, noting which evidence was weak and which appeared strong.

When discussing your hypotheses, do not assume that the data tell you more than they do. For instance, if we go back to the example in table 4.1 and look at country B, we may assume that unemployment could have contributed to civil unrest, but unless we gathered data on public opinion, media coverage of unemployment levels, and other related issues, we would only be guessing if we were to conclude that citizens were knowledgeable or highly concerned about this condition. Our point is that you should stick to analyzing the data that you have and be careful not to make assumptions you cannot support.

Once you have discussed individual variables and each of your hypotheses, you have finished the analysis section of your paper. Be sure to sum up your findings in a single sentence or two that can be used in your abstract. If you can do this, all that is left to complete your project is a relatively short conclusion section followed by the bibliography or reference list.

Note: You should always keep in mind that political scientists may disprove something in a case or cases, but we never prove anything. There are simply so many variables at work that we cannot explore all of them. We cannot know with absolute certainty that what we believe is correct is not influenced by other factors as well. Therefore, when writing up your analysis, it is acceptable to state, "The data disprove the hypotheses in this case," but it is not acceptable to write, "The data prove the hypotheses." In the latter case, you may say only that the data "support" the hypotheses.

THE CONCLUSION

The conclusion section of a research project is short, but students often find it difficult to write a conclusion if the analysis section contained a thorough discussion of the data and hypotheses. It is acceptable to use the conclusion section of your paper to discuss what you were unable to study or were unsure of at the completion of your project. For instance, you could discuss any reservations you may have concerning the strength of the relationships among your variables. You might also discuss alternative hypotheses that could be tested later. You might introduce additional questions that researchers could explore further or suggest how your study could be expanded to include other variables or other cases.

THE BIBLIOGRAPHY OR REFERENCE LIST

Your research paper should include a reference list or bibliography. Bibliographies and reference lists serve the same purpose but use different formats. In general, the reference list format is used if the author used parenthetical citations (as shown earlier in figure 4.2), and a bibliography is used if the author used footnotes. We provide some examples for citing some of the more complicated references in Part III of this text, but you should consult a style guide to develop this aspect of your paper.

FREQUENTLY ASKED QUESTIONS

"I have not had a methodology course, so how can I analyze my data?"
- Even if you cannot apply a sophisticated data analysis approach, you can still analyze the information you collect. If you have no formal methodological background, we suggest that you focus more on describing the data you collected than on making a hunch sound like a fact.
- The less methodological background you have, the more humble you should be in describing connections between variables. Use statements such as, "There appears to be . . ." or "The data indicate there may be. . . ."
- Never use the word "prove" or "proof" when describing findings, regardless of your method of analysis. Remember, you looked at only one or a few cases and only a limited number of variables. Again, humility is best.

"My hypothesis was wrong. Is that okay?"
- It's okay to be wrong as long as your hypothesis was based on variables selected with sound reasoning. In fact, showing that a well-developed hypothesis was not supported is often an interesting finding because it is surprising. Remember, we learn both from discovering that our hypotheses are correct and from finding them unsupported.

EXERCISES FOR CHAPTER 4

1. Choose a journal article abstract. As shown in figure 4.1, identify the following parts:
   a. the basis and structure of the study
   b. the "so what" response
   c. the methodology
   d. the most significant finding(s)

2. Choose a literature review within a scholarly article. Make a list of the different groupings or categories within it.
3. Choose a scholarly article that uses a case study methodology and print it out. With different colors of highlighters, mark the following sections:
   a. abstract
   b. introduction
   c. literature review
   d. research design (methodology)
   e. case presentation, analysis, and discussion of findings
   f. conclusions
   g. bibliography or reference list

Does the article's structure conform to the outline discussed in this chapter? Why or why not?

Project Resources

Part I of this text set out the structure of a question-based research project using a case-based methodology. Part II is designed to bridge the gap between knowing what to do and actually doing it. The chapters in this part provide specific guidance for question development, scholarly literature reviews, case selection, and data collection, thereby simplifying the process for developing a case-based research project.

Chapters 5–9 begin by establishing general questions that correspond to five specific topic areas in international relations: international conflict and security; U.S. foreign policy; international political economy; international organization and law; and globalization/global issues. You will also find several ideas for narrowing these general questions to more focused questions that can be used to define your unique project. Then we provide suggestions for where to begin your broad literature review, which will be vital in linking your study to others in the field.

As you read these chapters, keep in mind that while many students might choose the same or a similar question, what will make your paper individual and unique is your choice of case or cases. For example, a whole class may start with one question, but each student may develop a research design around different cases. To this end, we provide guidance for finding resources for case selection that will help you define your project.

In sum, Part II is designed to assist you in constructing the type of project outlined in Part I more efficiently. Chapters 5–9 provide ideas for project topics; citations for scholarly books, journal articles, and websites; and resources for case selection that will help you complete an interesting research project in international relations.

International Conflict and National Security

International conflict and national security are major themes associated with the study of international relations. Scholars and students are often interested in why international conflict exists and how it can be alleviated. Some choose to focus on the national security of the state while others pay more attention to the security of individuals or groups of people around the world. The most general question you can ask, therefore, when starting a question-based project is this:

What factors affect international conflict and national security?

One of the first things you might want to do is to read a bit about the history of war and conflict. The resources listed here are good starting places. Of course, you don't have to sit down and read reference works cover to cover. You may want to get an overview and then refer back to them for relevant information.

Resources on International Conflict

Brecher, Michael, and Jonathan Wilkenfeld. 1997. *A study of crisis*. Ann Arbor: University of Michigan Press.

Kaldor, Mary. 2007. *New and old wars*. 2nd ed. Cambridge: Polity Press.

Keegan, John. 1993. *A history of warfare*. New York: Random House.

Luttwak, Edward, and Stuart L. Koehl. 1991. *The dictionary of modern war*. New York: HarperCollins.

Nye, Joseph S. 2007. *Understanding international conflicts: An introduction to theory and history*. 6th ed. Longman Classics Series. New York: Longman.

O'Connell, Robert L. 1989. *Of arms and men: A history of war, weapons and aggression*. New York: Oxford University Press.

Stoessinger, John G. 2004. *Why nations go to war*. 9th ed. Boston: Bedford/St. Martin's Press.

Van Creveld, Martin. 1989. *Technology and war: From 2000 BC to the present*. New York: Free Press.

Once you have a background on conflict and war, you will need to narrow your question. In this chapter, we present just a few ways to do this.

TYPES OF CONFLICT

One way to narrow your topic is by narrowing the dependent variable— international conflict. Your textbook contains a lot of information about different types of conflict, different levels of violence, types of forces, and conflict resolution. These are areas that fall under the general theme of international conflict and military force.

One way to study conflict is to study a single type of conflict:

What factors affect [type of conflict]?

One text mentions six types of conflict:

- territorial border disputes
- conflicts over control of the government
- economic conflicts
- ethnic conflicts
- religious conflicts
- ideological conflicts (Goldstein 2003, 187)

So, one way to narrow your research question is to focus on one type of conflict. You might analyze, for example, under what conditions the international community gets involved in territorial border disputes by analyzing cases in which this has happened. Another example is to study under what conditions economic conflict occurs.

Suppose, for example, that you are interested in ethnic conflict. This type of conflict has increased greatly in the last decade, and some scholars have suggested that ethnic conflict will increase even more over time. Ethnic conflict has shaped many of the conflicts you know about from the news, including conflict in the former Yugoslavia and in Burundi, for example. You may begin with this question:

What factors contribute to ethnic conflict?

The next step is to determine two things:

1. What facet of ethnic conflict you will study
2. On which factors you will focus

Remember that the scholarly literature in the field of international relations is the most important resource you will use to determine the specification of your dependent variable (ethnic conflict) and your choice of independent variables (factors). For a full description of how to search the scholarly literature, see Chapter 2. Here are some citations that may be helpful as a starting place.

Resources on Different Types of Conflict

Brown, Michael E., Owen R. Cote, Jr., Sean M. Lynn-Jones, and Steven E. Miller, eds. 1997. *Nationalism and ethnic conflict*. Cambridge, MA: MIT Press.

Esman, Milton J. 1995. *Ethnic politics*. Ithaca, NY: Cornell University Press.

Griffiths, Stephen Iwan. 1993. *Nationalism and ethnic conflict*. New York: Oxford University Press.

Gurr, Ted Robert. 2000. *People versus states: Minorities at risk in the new century*. Washington, DC: United States Institute of Peace Press. [See especially pp. 65–95.]

Gurr, Ted Robert, and Barbara Harff. 1994. *Ethnic conflict in world politics*. Boulder, CO: Westview. [See especially Chapter 5, "A framework for analysis of ethnopolitical mobilization and conflict," pp. 77–96.]

Horowitz, Donald L. 1985. *Ethnic groups in conflict*. Berkeley: University of California Press.

Lobell, Steven. 2004. *Ethnic conflict and international politics: Explaining diffusion and escalation*. New York: Palgrave Macmillan.

Wolff, Stefan. 2006. *Ethnic conflict: A global perspective*. Oxford: Oxford University Press.

As you read about how political scientists have approached the question, you should develop a list of independent variables that are important in the literature. For example, Gurr and Harff (1994) identify external support and economic status as two key independent variables that affect the level of ethnic conflict. So, external support and economic status would go on your list of independent variables. The authors even set out how you might define these variables. For example, external support includes (1) verbal encouragement and advice, (2) financial support, (3) provision of intelligence information, (4) provision of safe havens for exiles and refugees, (5) mercenaries and military advisors, and (6) weaponry and supplies (Gurr and Harff 1994, 91). Think about how you would measure these characteristics of external support. You might measure financial support by the dollar amount of military and other aid, for example. See Chapter 3 for further elaboration. The key here is to be explicit about your variables and how you measure them.

Once you have completed your literature review (going well beyond the list of resources we presented) and have selected your independent variables, you must choose a case and develop hypotheses. (See Chapter 3.) Here are some sources that may help you develop a list of potential cases of ethnic conflict to study and provide you with information about particular cases.

Sources for Choosing Cases and Gathering Information

http://www.incore.ulst.ac.uk/ecrd/
> The Ethnic Conflict Research Digest publishes peer reviews of books, articles, and research papers on ethnic conflict. If you look at the top of this site, you will see a tab marked Resources. Under that is the Conflict Data Service. If you click on this, you will be able to access country-specific information.

http://mitpress.mit.edu/journals/inor/deibert-guide/section_4.html
> This site, hosted by MIT Press, has links to a number of other sites focused on ethnic conflict and nationalism.

http://www.cidcm.umd.edu/mar/
> The Minorities at Risk (MAR) Project contains data on 283 politically active ethnic groups. It contains information on group histories, risk assessments, and group chronologies for each group in the dataset.

LEVELS OF VIOLENCE

Another way to narrow the topic of international conflict and war is to study the scope of conflict or levels of violence.

What factors affect [level of violence]?

You may want to look at the levels of violence as defined by Goldstein:

- crisis
- guerrilla war
- terrorism
- coups/civil war
- limited war
- total war
- hegemonic war (Goldstein 2001, 234–35)

You can ask questions about conflicts of a particular violence level, for example:

What factors affect civil wars?

You will then have to do two things:

1. Specify exactly what aspect of civil wars you will study.
2. Identify the independent variables you will study.

The scholarly literature is your key to making these decisions. The resources listed here may help you start this process.

Resources on Civil Wars

Ali, Taisier M., and Robert O. Matthews, eds. 1999. *Civil wars in Africa: Roots and resolution*. Montreal: McGill-Queen's University Press.

Brown, Michael E., ed. 1996. *The international dimensions of internal conflict*. Cambridge, MA: MIT Press.

Collier, Paul and Nicholas Sambanis. 2005. *Understanding civil war: Evidence and analysis*. Washington, DC: World Bank Publications.

Kalyvas, Stathis N. 2001. "New" and "old" civil wars: A valid distinction? *World Politics* 54 (October): 99–118.

Zartman, I. William, ed. 1995. *Elusive peace: Negotiating an end to civil wars*. Washington, DC: The Brookings Institution.

Perhaps you are interested in the outbreak of civil war:

What factors affect the outbreak of civil war?

As you read the scholarly literature, you will make a list of independent variables that may be important. For example, Ali and Matthews suggest that there are at least three important variables you must study to understand why civil wars come about: (1) domestic socioeconomic structures (including differences in ethnic groups, politics, wealth distribution), (2) policies and practices of the ruling elite (failure/mismanagement by government), and (3) forces or events originating outside the country (1999, 4). These independent variables would go on your list. Brown identifies four sets of factors that would go on your list: structural factors, political factors, economic/social factors, and cultural/perceptual factors (1996, 13). He argues that bad leaders and bad neighbors trigger internal conflicts.

After you have developed your list of independent variables (derived from the literature), you can choose cases and develop hypotheses. (See Chapter 3.) Here are some sources that may help.

Sources for Choosing Cases and Gathering Information

http://www.crisisweb.org/home/index.cfm
> This is the website of the International Crisis Group (ICG), a private, multinational organization that works to prevent and contain conflict. The site includes links to information about a certain number of conflicts.

http://first.sipri.org/
> Facts on International Relations and Security Trends (FIRST) is a joint project of the International Relations and Security Network (ISN) and the Stockholm International Peace Research Institute (SIPRI). There are links at this website to databases that list conflicts by country or region (use advanced search for the region).

http://www.prio.no/CSCW/Datasets/Armed-Conflict/
> The Centre for the Study of Civil War (CSCW) in Oslo, Norway, has compiled a list of wars with intensity levels.

TYPES OF INTERVENTION

A different way to study conflict is to analyze state responses, or types of intervention associated with conflict.

What factors affect the type of intervention used by a state?

Intervention refers to actions by one state that affect another state. This type of question acknowledges that not all conflict is dealt with by using military means. A range of instruments and tools is available to states when in conflict. Nye, for example, gives a list of the following types of intervention and ranks them as less to more coercive:

- speeches
- broadcasts
- economic aid
- military advisors
- support to opposition
- blockade
- limited military action
- military invasion (2007, 62–63)

If you're interested in this topic, you will first need to read more generally on intervention.

Resources on Types of Intervention

Finnemore, Martha. 2003. *The purpose of intervention.* Ithaca, NY: Cornell University Press.

Huth, Paul K. 1998. Major power intervention in international crises, 1918–1988. *The Journal of Conflict Resolution* 42, no. 6: 744–70.

Jing, Chao, William H. Kaempfer, and Anton D. Lowenberg. 2003. Instrument choice and the effectiveness of international sanctions: A simultaneous equations approach. *Journal of Peace Research* 40, no. 5: 519–35.

Nye, Joseph. 2007. *Understanding international conflicts: An introduction to theory and history.* 6th ed. Longman Classic Series. New York: Longman.

Yoon, Mi Yung. 1997. Explaining U.S. intervention in third-world internal wars, 1945–1989. *The Journal of Conflict Resolution* 41, no. 4: 580–602.

To narrow your topic, you could ask a more specific question:

Under what conditions does a state use economic rather than military intervention?

Here you would have to turn to the scholarly literature for some possible conditions under which economic or military intervention would be more likely. Jing, Kaempfer, and Lowenberg (2003), for example, argue that military force is less likely when the target state is economically healthy and politically stable. Military action is more likely when a third country is assisting the target state and when the cost of economic sanctions is high. You might want to test these hypotheses in a case study. Remember that you would have to define and explain how you will measure all of the variables.

Sources for Choosing Cases and Gathering Information

http://webapp.icpsr.umich.edu/cocoon/ICPSR-STUDY/06035.xml
  This Inter-University Consortium for Political and Social Research (ICPSR) data collection on international military intervention, 1946–1988, is available for download if your university is a member of the consortium.

Tillema, Herbert K. 1994. Cold War alliance and overt military intervention, 1945–1991. *International Interactions* 20: 249–78.

ACTORS AND INTERSTATE CONFLICT

Another way to study international conflict is to focus on the actors involved. For example, do the characteristics associated with a state affect the likelihood that the state will go to war? These characteristics could include how powerful the state is; whether it is democratic or not; whether the state is undergoing political, economic, or social transformation; and so on. The broad question here becomes this:

What factors affect whether a state (or type of state) engages in military conflict?

First, you should read some broad works in this area. Here are just a few resources.

Resources on Interstate Conflict

Mansfield, Edward, and Jack Snyder. 2005. *Electing to fight: Why emerging democracies go to war*. Cambridge, MA: MIT Press.

Mearsheimer, John J. 2001. *The tragedy of great power politics*. New York: W. W. Norton and Company.

Rosecrance, Richard. 1987. *The rise of the trading state: Commerce and conquest in the modern world*. New York: Basic Books.

Rousseau, David. 2005. *Democracy and war: Institutions, norms, and the evolution of international conflict*. Stanford, CA: Stanford University Press.

Russett, Bruce. 1994. *Grasping the democratic peace*. Princeton, NJ: Princeton University Press.

Waltz, Kenneth N. 1979. *Theory of international politics*. New York: Longman.

After reading, if you are more interested in, for example, focusing on transitional states, you might ask a question like this:

Under what conditions does a state undergoing political transition go to war?

Here you might start with the work of Mansfield and Snyder (2005) and test their argument in cases that you develop. They argue, for example, that weak institutions will make it more likely that states undergoing transition will engage in military conflict. You may choose to focus on institutions such as the judicial system (i.e., the rule of law), the media, or the electoral system and then test whether and/or how these affected the likelihood of conflict in the cases you choose.

For your case studies, you will need to choose states in transition. In addition, you will need information on conflict so that you can see when and whether states in transition did or did not engage in military conflict.

Sources for Choosing Cases and Gathering Information

http://www.systemicpeace.org/polity/polity4.htm
   The Polity IV project contains information on political regime characteristics and transitions from 1800 to 2004.

http://www.systemicpeace.org/warlist.htm
   The website of the Center for Systemic Peace in Maryland lists major episodes of political violence.

CONFLICT RESOLUTION

Studies of international conflict are not confined to the factors that affect the outbreak of particular types of conflict or explanations about specific levels of violence. Research on international conflict can also focus on resolution:

What factors facilitate the resolution of conflict?

Many scholars are interested in how wars end after they start, and you may be, too. Some students are very interested in looking at under what conditions conflicts can actually be resolved, especially when conflict in the world seems all too prevalent. The first thing you should do if you want to research this area is to read generally about conflict resolution. Some good places to start (after your textbook and the *Journal of Conflict Resolution*) are listed here. Remember that you don't have to read every page of every book, but you must read enough to understand the important facets that scholars address in this field.

Resources on Conflict Resolution

Bar-Siman-Tov, Yaacov. 2004. *From conflict resolution to reconciliation.* New York: Oxford University Press.
Deutsch, Morton, Peter T. Coleman, and Eric Colton Marcus. 2006. *The handbook of conflict resolution: Theory and practice.* 2nd ed. Hoboken, NJ: John Wiley and Son.

Kurtz, Lester R., ed. 1999. *Encyclopedia of violence, peace, and conflict.* 3 vols. San Diego, CA: Academic Press.

Licklider, Roy, ed. 1993. *Stopping the killing: How civil wars end.* New York: New York University Press.

Pearson, Frederic. 2001. Dimensions of conflict resolution in ethnopolitical disputes. *Journal of Peace Research* 38, no. 3: 275–87.

Sandole, Dennis J. D., and Hugo van der Merwe. 1993. *Conflict resolution theory and practice: Integration and application.* New York: Manchester University Press.

Wallensteen, Peter. 2002. *Understanding conflict resolution: War, peace and the global system.* London: Sage.

Zartman, I. William, ed. 2007. *Peacemaking in international conflict: Methods and techniques.* 2nd ed. Washington, DC: United States Institute of Peace Press.

After you have a basic understanding of conflict resolution, you will have to narrow your question. One way to do this is to focus on particular actors' roles in conflict resolution:

Under what conditions does [a particular actor] affect the resolution of conflict?

These actors may include the following:

- international organizations
- states
- peacekeeping troops
- nongovernmental organizations
- individuals

Let's take the case of peacekeeping troops. This is a relatively new area for research in international security and conflict resolution. The United Nations (UN) has expanded peacekeeping in the last two decades, and this has become an interesting area for research. In fact, the UN peacekeeping forces won the 1988 Nobel Peace Prize for their efforts. Peacekeeping has raised a number of issues of importance to international relations, and you might want to focus on this facet of conflict resolution:

Under what conditions do peacekeeping forces affect the resolution of conflict?

You will next have to do two things:

1. Specify exactly what you mean by the resolution of conflict.
2. Identify the conditions you will study.

It is time to consult the scholarly literature for help with this. After rereading your textbook, you can turn to a number of recent works for additional information.

Resources on Peacekeeping Forces

Articles within the academic journal *International Peacekeeping*.

Diehl, Paul F., Daniel Druckman, and James Wall. 1998. International peacekeeping and conflict resolution: A taxonomic analysis with implications. *Journal of Conflict Resolution* 42 (February): 33–55.

Dobson, Hugo. 2003. *Japan and UN peacekeeping: New pressures and new responses.* London: Routledge.

Durch, William J., ed. 1993. *The evolution of UN peacekeeping: Case studies and comparative analysis.* New York: St. Martin's Press.

MacQueen, Norrie. 2002. *United Nations peacekeeping in Africa since 1960.* London: Longman.

Mayall, James, ed. 1996. *The new interventionism, 1991–1994: United Nations experience in Cambodia, former Yugoslavia, and Somalia.* New York: Cambridge University Press.

Pushkina, Darya. 2006. A recipe for success? Ingredients of a successful peacekeeping mission. *International Peacekeeping* 13(2): 133–149.

Ratner, Steven R. 1996. *The new UN peacekeeping: Building peace in lands of conflict after the Cold War.* New York: St. Martin's Press.

As you do your reading on peacekeeping, make sure you look for the independent variables (factors) the authors suggest are important to understanding the topic. Durch (1993), for example, sets out three important variables to study: (1) local consent, (2) the support of the United States and Great Powers, and (3) a desire by combatants to salvage something rather than to win at all costs. Other scholars will present a perhaps slightly altered list of important characteristics.

Once you have a list of independent variables, you can choose cases and develop hypotheses. (See Chapter 3.) In the case of peacekeeping, it is very easy to get a list of the UN peacekeeping missions. The UN has an elaborate website with very specific information on and documentation of peacekeeping missions.

Sources for Choosing Cases and Gathering Information

http://www.un.org/peace/index.html
    You can find UN data at this United Nations' UN's website. From this page, click on links about peacekeeping.

http://www.brad.ac.uk/acad/confres/monitor/
    This Index to UN and Conflict Monitor site contains links to reports on UN peacekeeping operations.

TERRORISM

Many students today are interested in the topic of international terrorism, and this general topic clearly falls under the rubric of international conflict. There are many ways you could develop a question-based research project around the general topic of terrorism. Generally, you might ask the following:

What factors affect terrorism?

If you start here, you will need to do two things:

1. Specify the facet of terrorism you will study.
2. Identify the independent variables you will study.

After reading your textbook, you may want to consult some more references on terrorism. Some suggestions are listed here.

Resources on Terrorism

Combs, Cindy. 1997. *Terrorism in the twenty-first century*. Upper Saddle River, NJ: Prentice Hall.

Hoffman, Bruce. 2006. *Inside terrorism*, 2nd ed. New York: Columbia University Press.

Nacos, Bridgette Lebens. 2007. Mass-mediated terrorism: The central role of the media in terrorism and counterterrorism. New York: Routledge.

Oliverio, Annamarie. 1998. *The state of terror*. Albany: SUNY Press.

Rapoport, David C., ed. 1988. *Inside terrorist organizations*. New York: Columbia University Press.

Reich, Walter, ed. 1990. *Origins of terrorism: Psychologies, ideologies, theologies, states of mind*. New York: Cambridge University Press. [See especially Chapter 13, "Questions to be answered, research to be done, knowledge to be applied," by Martha Crenshaw, pp. 247–60, and Chapter 14, "Understanding terrorist behavior: The limits and opportunities of psychological inquiry," by Walter Reich, pp. 261–80.]

Thackrah, John. 2004. *Dictionary of terrorism*. London: Routledge.

Whittacker, David J. 2007. *Terrorism: Understanding the global threat*, 2nd ed. New York: Longman/Pearson.

Suppose that, after reading about terrorism, you are interested in the factors that lead to the end of terrorist organizations:

Under what conditions do terrorist organizations disband or end their terrorist ways?

Not many scholars have addressed the issue of why terrorist organizations cease to exist, but the United States Institute of Peace held a conference on how terrorism ends, and you can go to http://www.usip.org/pubs/specialreports/sr990525.html to get an overview of the proceedings. Professor Martha Crenshaw argues that a number of independent variables are important to consider, including (1) factors related to the terrorist groups themselves and (2) the tools governments use to combat terrorism. As you read the scholarly literature, you can look for those independent variables that other scholars suggest would explain the end of a terrorist organization or its violent actions. Also, make sure that you define what you mean by a terrorist group. Remember that definitions may vary, and you must be clear about your definition.

Once you have a list of independent variables, it's time to choose cases and develop hypotheses. (See Chapter 3.) A growing number of good websites offer information on terrorism and terrorist organizations.

Sources for Choosing Cases and Gathering Information

http://www.usip.org/library/topics/terrorism.html
> The United States Institute of Peace has a site on terrorism with links to a number of different sources. Look for links to research studies and projects for additional information.

http://wits.nctc.gov/FederalDiscoverWITS/index.do?N=0
> National Counterterrorism Center, *Worldwide Incidents Tracking System*

http://www.state.gov/s/ct/rls/crt/
> *Patterns of Global Terrorism* is a report from the U.S. Department of State. It is intended to provide a record for those countries and groups involved in international terrorism.

http://www.start.umd.edu/start/
> National Consortium for the Study of Terrorism and Responses to Terrorism.

GENERAL DATA SOURCES FOR CHOOSING CASES AND GATHERING EVIDENCE

The following sources will help you gather information on conflict and international security.

Websites

http://www.isn.ethz.ch/
> The International Relations and Security Network (ISN) website was developed by the Center for Security Studies and Conflict Research, ETH Zurich. Look under Resources and Publications for information on conflict and security.

http://first.sipri.org/
> Facts on International Relations and Security Trends (FIRST) is a joint project of the International Relations and Security Network (ISN) and the Stockholm International Peace Research Institute (SIPRI). It contains databases on information related to conflict and international relations.

http://mitpress.mit.edu/journals/INOR/deibert-guide/TOC.html
This site, created by Ronald J. Deibert of the University of Toronto, is a good source with links on individual countries and ethnic conflict.

http://www.lib.umich.edu/govdocs/psintl.html
The University of Michigan has an excellent site. This page has a section on peace and security.

Publications

Bercovitch, Jacob, and Richard Jackson. 1997. *International conflict: A chronological encyclopedia of conflicts and their management 1945–1995*. Washington, DC: Congressional Quarterly. [This book contains a listing of conflicts, plus citations for further reference for each conflict.]

Shanty, Frank, and Raymond Picquet. 2003. *Encyclopedia of world terrorism*. Armonk, NY: Sharpe Reference.

U.S. Foreign Policy

Many students are interested in the study of foreign policy and want to do research papers on this topic. The study of foreign policy is the study of how policy decisions about international relations are made. So, the broadest question you might ask about foreign policy is this:

What factors affect foreign policy decision making?

There are a number of ways to narrow this topic for a suitable research paper in international relations. This chapter discusses a few approaches you could take. First, however, you must know about foreign policy more generally. After reviewing your textbook, you might look at some of the following resources.

Resources on Foreign Policy

Herrick, Christopher, and Patricia B. McRae. 2003. *Issues in American foreign policy*. New York: Longman.

Ikenberry, G. John, ed. 2004. *American foreign policy: Theoretical essays.* New York: Longman.

Neack, Laura, Jeanne A. K. Hey, and Patrick J. Haney. 1995. *Foreign policy analysis: Continuity and change in its second generation*. Englewood Cliffs, NJ: Prentice Hall.

Nye, Joseph. 2010. *Soft power and U.S. foreign policy: Theoretical, historical and contemporary perspectives*. New York: Routledge.

Skidmore, David, and Valerie M. Hudson. 1993. *The limits of state autonomy: Societal groups and foreign policy formation*. Boulder, CO: Westview Press.

One of the ways to narrow a question about foreign policy is to more narrowly define the dependent variable—in this case, foreign policy decision making. For example, you could focus on a particular issue area of foreign policy:

What factors affect foreign policy decision making in the realm of [issue]?

Issue areas you might consider include the following:

- conflict (e.g., the decision to go to war, how to respond to a crisis)
- international economics (e.g., the decision to pursue trade agreements)
- environment (e.g., the decision to pursue international environmental agreements)
- human rights (e.g., the decision to link human rights violations in other countries to foreign aid)

Even if you narrow the dependent variable, you will need to narrow your question further. In this chapter, we discuss two broad ways to do this—by focusing on individual characteristics of leaders and by focusing on state-level explanations.

INDIVIDUAL CHARACTERISTICS

One way to do so is to analyze how individuals make foreign policy decisions. Some scholars assume rationality on the part of leaders; that is, they study foreign policy decisions as if individual leaders are interchangeable. Other scholars focus on differences in individual decision makers, looking at the motivations, beliefs, values, perceptions, and misperceptions of decision makers. While you may read a lot about this in your textbook, it is often very difficult to research the psychological makeup of individuals. Remember that you will need *evidence* for all of your cases, and it may be hard to get that evidence. For example, you may hypothesize that President George W. Bush's foreign policy making was affected by his upbringing. However, you may not have the evidence you need to support that argument. If you are going to attempt to analyze individual decision makers, you will have to do so in a systematic way. Your question then becomes:

What individual factors affect a leader's foreign policy decision making?

You will next turn to the scholarly literature to identify the independent variables you will study. Here is a list of concepts followed by important citations for resources that may help you in explaining foreign policy decision making that deviates from what would be expected if leaders acted only rationally.

Perception: The decision maker's images of reality may shape the decisions reached.

Jervis, Robert. 1976. *Perception and misperception in international politics.* Princeton, NJ: Princeton University Press.

Vertzberger Yaacov. 1990. *The world in their minds: Information processing, cognition, and perception in foreign policy decision-making.* Stanford: Stanford University Press.

Operational code: A set of perceptions and beliefs shapes how leaders will respond and act.

Walker, Stephen G., Mark Schafer, and Michael D. Young. 1998. Systematic procedures for operational code analysis: Measuring and modeling Jimmy Carter's operational code. *International Studies Quarterly* 42 (March): 175–89.

Personality: Characteristics of the individual shape the way she or he makes decisions.

Byman, Daniel L., and Kenneth M. Pollack. 2001. Let us now praise great men: Bringing the statesman back in. *International Security* 25(4): 107–46.

George, Alexander L., and Juliette L. George. 1964. *Woodrow Wilson and Colonel House: A personality study.* New York: Dover Publications.

Hermann, Margaret G. 1980. Explaining foreign policy behavior using the personal characteristics of political leaders. *International Studies Quarterly* 24 (March): 7–46.

Prospect theory: Individuals tend to be cautious when they are in a good position and more likely to take risks when they are in a bad position; therefore, understanding differences in risk assessment is key to understanding the outcome of decisions.

Levy, Jack. 1997. Prospect theory, rational choice, and international relations. *International Studies Quarterly* 41 (March): 87–112.

McDermott, Rose. 1998. *Risk-taking in international politics: Prospect theory in American foreign policy.* Ann Arbor: University of Michigan Press.

McDermott Rose. 2004. Prospect theory in political science: Gains and losses from the first decade. *Political Psychology* 25(2): 289–312.

By considering individual characteristics, you can also narrow your question in a slightly different manner:

Under what conditions do [individual characteristics] affect a leader's foreign policy making?

This type of question may focus on one characteristic of the leader and ask about the conditions under which this characteristic affects foreign policy decision making.

Take, for example, this more specific question:

Under what conditions does a leader's understanding of history (i.e., historical lessons) affect his or her foreign policy making?

This question addresses how leaders use their own understanding of history to inform and shape their present foreign policy choices. Your textbook probably talks about historical lessons and foreign policy making. It may discuss the Vietnam Syndrome, for example, which suggests that foreign policy decisions today are made to avoid the perceived problems associated with the American war in Vietnam in the 1960s and early 1970s. If you develop this research project, you first need to reread what your textbook says about historical lessons and foreign policy. Then go beyond your text to read more about the concept from some of the good resources available.

Resources on Historical Lessons

Khong, Yuen Foong. 1992. *Analogies at war: Korea, Munich, Dien Bien Phu, and the Vietnam decisions of 1965.* Princeton, NJ: Princeton University Press.

Neustadt, Richard, and Ernest R. May. 1986. *Thinking in time: The uses of history for decision makers.* New York: Macmillan USA.

Simons, Geoffrey. 1998. *Vietnam syndrome: Impact on U.S. foreign policy.* New York: St. Martin's.

Taylor, Andrew J., and John T. Rourke. 1995. Historical analogies in the congressional foreign policy process. *Journal of Politics* 57 (May): 460–68.

Vertzberger, Yaacov Y. I. 1990. *The world in their minds: Information processing, cognition, and perception in foreign policy decision-making.* Stanford, CA: Stanford University Press. [See especially pp. 298–308.]

After you understand something about the concept of historical lessons or analogies, you will need to pick your case or cases and develop your hypotheses. You may analyze two foreign policy decisions to understand the conditions under which a particular leader uses historical lessons, or you may compare different leaders to see if and when they use historical lessons differently or similarly. A different project would focus on the different ways historical lessons are used. For example, Vertzberger (1990) argues that leaders can use historical lessons in four ways:

1. to define the situation
2. to circumscribe roles
3. to determine strategy
4. to justify strategy

You might develop hypotheses that suggest under what conditions a leader will use historical lessons to justify strategy, for example.

For this type of analysis, you will need a good understanding of the foreign policy decisions themselves and then good information (data) about how leaders use historical lessons. You will need to analyze leadership speeches, interviews, and policy pronouncements in a systematic way. Don't simply pick a few speeches to make an assertion about how the leader uses historical lessons. Memoirs are also a good source for information on individual leaders' perceptions and views. In addition to the following sources, see the related websites listed under general sources at the end of this chapter.

Sources for Choosing Cases and Gathering Information

http://www.archives.gov/presidential-libraries/research/
  This website gives information on finding speeches and writings by American presidents through presidential libraries.

http://www.archives.gov/
  The U.S. National Archives website contains links to information on American political leaders.

http://millercenter.org/scripps/archive/speeches
  The Miller Center of Public Affairs at the University of Virginia has an online presidential speech archive.

STATE-LEVEL ANALYSES

Another way to further narrow the more general question about foreign policy making is to focus on state-level independent variables. State-level analyses center on the role of domestic politics and groups in the process of making foreign policy. The question here is this:

What state-level factors affect foreign policy?

State-level factors include important domestic political actors such as:

- governmental bureaucracies, including the military
- domestic interest groups
- the public

State-level factors also include the political system (e.g., authoritarian versus democratic).

To do research on domestic groups and foreign policy making, you need to be able to obtain the information that you need. If you are developing a research paper that includes analysis of a certain governmental bureaucracy, for example, you will need access to information about how this organization operates. (We'll expand on this with some specific examples soon.) If you are doing a paper on comparative foreign policy (i.e., foreign policy making in different political systems), you will need information about policies and the political system in all of the countries you will be comparing. Language skills can help significantly in this endeavor.

Bureaucratic Politics

Suppose that you are interested in how governmental bureaucracies affect foreign policy:

Under what conditions do governmental bureaucracies affect foreign policy decision making?

When you look at the general information on foreign policy, you will undoubtedly find some mention of bureaucratic politics. Bureaucratic models (sometimes called governmental politics models) suggest that foreign policy decisions are the result of bargaining among government agencies that usually have different interests. For example, the State Department may have different interests than the Defense Department, and foreign policy recommendations may reflect bargaining about those differences. Some works that discuss this in more detail include those listed here.

Resources on Bureaucratic Politics

Allison, Graham T., and Philip Zelikow. 1999. *Essence of decision: Explaining the Cuban missile crisis.* 2nd ed. New York: Longman.

Bendor, Jonathan, and Thomas H. Hammond. 1992. Rethinking Allison's models. *American Political Science Review* 86 (June): 301–22.

Welch, David A. 1992. The organizational process and bureaucratic politics paradigms: Retrospect and prospect. *International Security* 17 (Autumn): 112–46.

After reading Allison and Zelikow (1999), for example, you will more fully understand the bureaucratic model of foreign policy making. The bureaucratic model focuses attention on bargaining among different political players over policy outcomes. Here you need to pay attention to (1) who is involved in the bargaining, (2) what factors shape perceptions and preferences for each of those involved, (3) how different views are presented, and (4) how the final decision is made.

The next step in the process is choosing your case or cases and developing hypotheses. You can approach this in a number of ways. First, you can do what Allison and Zelikow (1999) did—choose one very important crisis and analyze the conditions under which bureaucratic politics affected decision making during that crisis. Another way to approach this would be to analyze different or contradictory foreign policy decisions made in one specific issue area during the same administration. Likewise, you may develop a research plan that studies similar foreign policy decisions made under different administrations with different preferences. In order to choose cases, you will have to read broadly about different foreign policy decisions. Then you will be able to make some choices about which cases to study and hypotheses to develop.

After you choose your cases, you will need to do more research on them. To continue with our example, what kind of evidence do you need in order to answer questions about bureaucratic politics? For a bureaucratic model, you need to focus on the interaction of various players representing various interests. And if you are going to study bureaucratic politics, you will need to have access to records that show the interaction of these various players. Therefore, it is crucial to make sure that you choose a case about which there is an ample amount of material; for example, transcripts of meetings among top players. Memoirs by participants can be helpful in understanding the decision-making process. Be careful, however, that you take memoirs for what they are: one participant's recollection of what occurred. Others may have a very different perspective.

Once you have information, you will need to make the connection between the information you collect and foreign policy decision making itself. This is where you need to be explicit about the connections. For example, you may have researched the interests of the CIA, for example, but you need to be explicit about how these interests were articulated and how they did or did not affect decision making. Don't take for granted that your reader will see and understand the connections—make them explicit. Also, you need to remember that a focus on bureaucracy may help you understand foreign policy decision making, but it will certainly not explain everything about why a particular decision was or was not made. This is because other political actors may have some effect on foreign policy making. Be careful—don't make sweeping generalizations that you cannot support.

Source for Choosing Cases and Gathering Information
http://www.lib.lsu.edu/gov/
> This website provides a list of U.S. executive agencies and links, including those related to the Department of Defense, the Department of State, the Department of the Air Force, the Department of the Navy, the Department of the Army, and the United States Marine Corps.

Public Opinion
Suppose that you are interested not in the bureaucracy but in public opinion:

Under what conditions does public opinion influence foreign policy decisions?
The public's role in foreign policy making may be a research area that interests you. Much has been written about the important role of public opinion in domestic policy making, but there has been more of a debate about whether and when public opinion matters in foreign policy making. Here you might look at public opinion survey results on specific foreign policy issues to see whether political leaders change their own positions on issues before or after a change in public opinion or not at all. You will also need evidence to suggest that there is a relationship if, indeed, you do find that there is a change in policy when public opinion changes. You need survey data and a way to measure changes in leaders' positions or policies. Some sources to start with are listed here.

Resources on Public Opinion
Entman, Robert M. 2004. *Projections of power: Framing news, public opinion, and U.S. foreign policy.* Chicago: University of Chicago Press.
Graham, Thomas. 1994. Public opinion and U.S. foreign policy decision making. In *The new politics of American foreign policy*, ed. David A. Deese, 190–215. New York: St. Martin's Press.

Holsti, Ole R. 1996 and 2009 rev. ed. *Public opinion and American foreign policy*. Ann Arbor: University of Michigan Press.

Mueller, John. 1994. *Policy and opinion in the Gulf War*. Chicago: University of Chicago Press.

Powlick, Philip J., and Andrew Z. Katz. 1998. Defining the American public opinion/foreign policy nexus. *International Studies Quarterly* 42 (May): 29–63.

Shapiro, Robert Y., and Benjamin I. Page. 1994. Foreign policy and public opinion. In *The new politics of American foreign policy*, ed. David A. Deese, 216–35. New York: St. Martin's Press.

Western, Jon W. 2005. *Selling intervention and war: The presidency, the media, and the American public*. Baltimore: Johns Hopkins University Press.

Of course, you will not be conducting public opinion surveys yourself, but you can use survey data that has already been compiled and is available to students and scholars. Even if you cannot do sophisticated statistical analysis, you can look at survey data for trends over time. Holsti (1996, 197), in his final chapter, sets out potentially fruitful research paths, suggesting that you look at the role of public opinion by (1) the type of issue, (2) the stage of the policy process, and/or (3) the decision makers' beliefs about public opinion. Types of issues that may be of interest are trade, the environment, and ethnic, racial, religious, and nationalist conflicts and civil wars (Holsti 1996, 193–94). If you consider the stage of the policy process, you can study steps in policy making, as Graham (1994) did in the case of arms control: agenda setting, negotiation, ratification, and implementation. For beginning researchers, the fourth area may be somewhat easier to study. You would need to look at what a particular leader says he or she believes about public opinion and then compare that to actual decisions to see if you can establish a connection or pattern.

As another option, you might want to research the factors that affect public opinion itself.

What factors affect public opinion on foreign policy issues?

Note that the dependent variable here has changed from foreign policy making to public opinion.

Once you understand something about public opinion and foreign policy making and have decided, more specifically, what you would like to study, you are ready to choose independent variables and cases and to develop hypotheses. If, for example, you want to compare the role of public opinion by type of issue, you may choose to look at a few decisions in one issue area, or you may choose to compare decisions across issue areas. You must be explicit about why you choose the cases you do. In all likelihood, the data you will need will include a measurement of public opinion. Sources for this are listed below. You will also need information on foreign policy decisions themselves.

Then you must take the next step and make a connection, if possible, between public opinion and decisions made. Remember that you cannot *conclusively* show that public opinion had a particular effect on any specific decision. However, you can say either that there was no relationship or that there may be a relationship. As you continue in your international relations studies, you will learn more sophisticated ways to determine the likelihood that there is a relationship at work.

Sources for Choosing Cases and Gathering Information

http://libraries.ucsd.edu/ssds/pubpolls.html
> This website gives an overview of resources for the study of public opinion.

http://www.ala.org/ala/mgrps/divs/acrl/publications/crlnews/2006/oct/opinionpoll.cfm
> The Association of College and Research Libraries has developed a guide that lists public opinion poll websites.

http://pewglobal.org/
> The Pew Research Center has a site for international public opinion information.

Public Opinion Quarterly
> This scholarly journal is an excellent source for research on public opinion.

http://wikis.ala.org/acrl/index.php/Guide_to_Public_Opinion_Poll_Web_Sites
> Association of College and Research Libraries listing of public opinion websites.

Interest Groups

If you are interested in the role of different state-level actors in the foreign policy process, you may choose to design a different type of project. For example, you might ask this question:

What factors affect the strategies of interest groups?

Many students are interested in how interest groups affect policy making, but it is very difficult to ascertain the degree to which interest groups affect policy making. This question basically asks about the strategies of different types of interest groups to see if there is evidence that suggests a pattern in how interest groups function. Note that the dependent variable is not foreign policy making or foreign policy. The dependent variable is the strategies of interest groups. A good place to start is to read about interest groups and the process of foreign policy making. First, reread your textbook, and then go beyond that. The following resources may help.

Resources on Interest Groups

Crabb, Cecil V., Jr., Glenn J. Antizzo, and Leila E. Sarieddine. 2000. *Congress and the foreign policy process: Modes of legislative behavior.* Baton Rouge: Louisiana State University Press. [See especially pp. 137–55.]

Hudson, V. M., S. M. Sims, and J. C. Thomas. 1993. The domestic political context of foreign policy-making: Explicating a theoretical construct. In *The limits of state autonomy,* ed. D. Skidmore and V. M. Hudson, 49–101. Boulder, CO: Westview.

Jentleson, Bruce W. 2004. *American foreign policy: The dynamics of choice in the twenty-first century.* New York: W. W. Norton. [See especially pp. 44–47.]

Wittkopf, Eugene, and James McCormick. 2004. *The domestic sources of American foreign policy: Insights and evidence.* Lanham, MD: Rowman and Littlefield.

After doing this background reading, you can focus more closely on the types and strategies of interest groups. Jentleson (2004), for example, sets out a list of types of interest groups, including economic groups, identity groups (religious or ethnic), political issue groups, state and local governments, and foreign governments. He also sets out four strategies: (1) influencing Congress, (2) influencing the executive branch, (3) influencing public opinion, and (4) corruption (e.g., bribing, giving gifts, etc.). Based on this material, you can design your research plan in a number of different ways.

- Study one major foreign policy decision and the factors that shaped interest group strategies.
- Study one type of group to see if its strategies changed over time.
- Study foreign policy decisions about the same issue to see how and why an interest group's strategies changed over time.

Once you choose your cases, you will need to find out exactly what strategies the interest group or groups used. Then you will need specific information about the interest group's activities so you can group them by strategy. For example, you might consider mailings to the public to be a strategy to influence public opinion. Meetings with congressional representatives fall under the category of influencing Congress. You can obtain information about interest group activities in part from the interest group itself. Don't rely on this alone, however. You'll need more information from the press and secondary sources.

Sources for Choosing Cases and Gathering Information

http://www.lib.umich.edu/govdocs/psusp.html#lobby

The University of Michigan has a good collection of sources on lobbying and interest groups. This site contains links to information about groups and their sites.

http://www.opensecrets.org/lobbyists/index.asp

The Center for Responsive Politics has a website that contains a database of lobbying groups. You can search by category or for a particular group. If you look in a section on ideological or single issues, you will find a category for foreign and defense policy.

http://www.opensecrets.org/industries/indus.php?ind=Q04

The Open Secrets website includes information on interest groups in the foreign policy sector.

Terrorism

U.S. foreign policy related to terrorism has been an important topic for quite some time and certainly since 9/11/2001. Many students are interested in foreign policy in this area. One way to approach this general topic is to compare changes

- over time
- under different presidents
- in regard to different foreign countries.

Your general research question would be:

What factors affect U.S. foreign policy on terrorism?

If you are interested in this question, you must first read what scholars have written on the general topic.

Resources on Terrorism and U.S. Foreign Policy

Entman, Robert. 2004. *Projections of power: Framing news, public opinion, and foreign policy.* Chicago: University of Chicago Press.

Lynch, Timothy J., Robert S. Singh. 2008. *After Bush: The case for continuity in American foreign policy.* Cambridge: Cambridge University Press.

Nacos, Bridgette L. 2007. *Mass-mediated terrorism: The central role of the media in terrorism and counterterrorism.* Lanham, MD: Rowman & Littlefield.

Pillar, Paul R. 2003. *Terrorism and U.S. foreign policy.* Washington, DC: Brookings Institution Press.

After reading about terrorism and foreign policy in a post-9/11 environment, you might want to assess the differences and similarities in U.S. foreign policy on terrorism between the presidencies of George Bush and Barack Obama. One way to do this would be to take Lynch and Singh's argument that American foreign policy under President Obama would show significant continuity with that of President Bush. First you would have to determine what specific policies you will study. Second, you must determine the degree to which this is continuity or change from one presidency to the others. Finally, you must address the factors that affect that continuity or change.

Sources for Choosing Cases and Gathering Information

http://www.start.umd.edu/start/
> National Consortium for the Study of Terrorism and Responses to Terrorism.

http://people.haverford.edu/bmendels/
> Global Terrorism Resource Database—developed at Haverford College.

GENERAL DATA SOURCES FOR CHOOSING CASES AND GATHERING EVIDENCE

The following sources will help you gather information on foreign policy.

For Domestic and Foreign Policies and the President

Public Papers of the President. Washington, DC: Federal Register Division, National Archives and Records Service, General Services Administration.

Each *Public Papers* volume contains the papers and speeches of the president of the United States that were issued by the Office of the Press Secretary during the specified time period.

Government Documents

http://www.gpoaccess.gov/index.html
> This government site provides access to U.S. government documents.

Websites for Foreign Policy Resources

http://www.lib.umich.edu/govdocs/forpol.html
> The University of Michigan has an incredible site that contains a whole section on U.S. foreign policy. The section is divided into the following categories: Congress, declassified material, the executive branch, laws, the president, regulations, and website indexes.

http://www.mtholyoke.edu/acad/intrel/feros-pg.htm
> Professor Vincent Ferraro of Mount Holyoke College has created an excellent site that contains a whole section on documents. Within it is a broad range of American foreign policy documents.

http://wsrv.clas.virginia.edu/~rjb3v/usgovt.html
> This award-winning site lists resources for the study of foreign affairs.

International Political Economy

A rich subject for research in international relations is the area of international political economy (IPE). Issues in IPE include trade and money, North–South relations, economic parameters of power, and the role of international actors in the IPE. Also included in this area are issues related to economic integration in regions around the world. In this chapter, we discuss two ways to narrow questions about these topics by focusing on:

- what international actors do or how they behave in the international economy
- how international economic policies or decisions affect people

The relationship between international politics and economics is a growing and important area of study, but it is sometimes difficult for students to develop a research paper in this area without a substantial academic base in economics; however, there are areas that you can explore, and we focus on these in this chapter.

IPE AND THE ROLE OF INTERNATIONAL ACTORS

A number of international actors are involved in the IPE, and you may be interested in doing research on them. These actors include the following:

- states
- political leaders
- multinational corporations (MNCs)
- international governmental organizations (IGOs)
- nongovernmental organizations (NGOs)

As your textbook probably explains, one of the important issues here is to what degree sovereignty is diminished by growing international economic interdependence and with what results. The first step in researching international actors' roles in the IPE is to understand what your textbook says about

IPE. You then will want to turn to other works for your general literature review. Some suggestions are offered here.

Resources on IPE

Abdelal, Rawi, Mark Blyth, and Craig Parsons. 2010. *Constructing the international economy.* Ithaca: Cornell University Press.

Caporaso, James A., and David P. Levine. 1993. *Theories of political economy.* New York: Cambridge University Press.

Cohn, Theodore. 2003. *Global political economy: Theory and practice.* New York: Longman.

Gilpin, Robert. 1987. *The political economy of international relations.* Princeton, NJ: Princeton University Press.

————. 2003. *Global political economy: Understanding the international economic order.* New Delhi: Orient Longman.

Grieco, Joseph, and G. John Ikenberry. 2003. *State power and world markets.* New York: W. W. Norton and Co.

Rodrick, Dani. 2008. *One economics, many recipes: Globalization, institutions, and economic growth.* Princeton: Princeton University Press.

Weiss, Linda, ed. 2003. *States in the global economy: Bringing domestic institutions back in.* Cambridge: Cambridge University Press.

One of the challenges for a student who wishes to do research on international actors and IPE is the lack of knowledge you may have about economics. That said, suppose that you want to research the following question on one type of international actor:

What factors affect the participation of [international actor] in international economics?

Note that in this question the dependent variable is the participation of the international actor—not IPE per se. If you choose this more focused question, you will be directing your attention to political and economic factors that affect how important actors behave in areas related to international economics.

Multinational Corporations

Suppose that you are interested in multinational corporations. Through your preliminary reading, you will find that governments often intervene in the rules for MNCs. You might then ask this question:

Under what conditions do governments intervene in the rules for MNCs?

To begin this type of research, you will need to reread your textbook and understand that there is a debate about the role of MNCs in the IPE. After that, you will need to pursue your general literature review by focusing on MNCs. You may want to turn to the resources listed here for a start.

Resources on MNCs

Doremus, Paul N., William W. Keller, Louis W. Pauly, and Simon Reich. 1998. *The myth of the global corporation.* Princeton, NJ: Princeton University Press.

Gilpin, Robert. 1975. *U.S. power and the multinational corporation.* New York: Basic Books.

Jensen, Nathan Michael. 2006. *Nation-states and the multinational corporation: A political economy of foreign direct investment.* Princeton: Princeton University Press.

Poynter, Thomas A. 1985. *Multinational enterprises and government intervention.* New York: St. Martin's Press. [See especially Chapter 3, "The basis of intervention."]

Saari, David J. 1999. *Global corporations and sovereign nations: Collision or cooperation?* Westport, CT: Quorum Books/Greenwood Publishing Group.

Sally, Razeen. 1995. *States and firms: Multinational enterprises in institutional competition.* New York: Routledge.

There are a number of ways to study the conditions under which governments intervene in the practices of MNCs. First, you must define intervention. Poynter defines intervention as "forced sharing of the benefits (economic mostly) generated by the subsidiary" (1985, 36). You may choose to use this definition of intervention, giving Poynter proper credit, of course. You must then choose independent variables and case(s) and develop hypotheses. For example, you may choose independent variables such as the characteristics of the subsidiary within the country or host-nation characteristics.

You could choose cases in a number of ways. One is to study one business sector and look for differences in how the government deals with individual subsidiaries. Another way is to look across business sectors. The following sources give you some starting points.

Sources for Choosing Cases and Gathering Information

http://www.kompass.com
  This site allows you to search by region and industry. It contains information on 1.6 million companies worldwide.

http://tcc.export.gov/index.asp
  The U.S. Department of Commerce's Trade Compliance Center site allows you to search by country for trade policies.

The World Trade Organization

Another way to narrow a question about international actors is to choose a specific organization on which to focus. For example, you may want to study the World Trade Organization (WTO). This multinational IGO "promotes, monitors, and adjudicates international trade" (Goldstein 2003, 329) and has caused much controversy since its birth in 1995 from the General Agreement on Tariffs and Trade (GATT). Even if you do not have a strong background in economics, you still can study the WTO. One approach is to study media coverage of the WTO. Another is to study how opposition groups in different countries behave:

Under what conditions do groups protest the WTO?

First, read more about the WTO. Remember, however, that as a political scientist you need to keep an open mind. You may already have an opinion about the WTO, but a well-designed research project may lead to unexpected conclusions. For example, if you think the protesters are all a bunch of radical loudmouths, you may be surprised by the range of different groups involved and the issues on the table. Likewise, you may believe that the governments involved in the negotiations are greedy and do not have the best interests of their people in mind. However, you may not find this to be true. Be open to a complicated set of relationships. As you pursue your literature review, you may want to look at the following resources.

Resources on the WTO

Blustein, Paul. 2009. *Misadventures of the most favored nations: Clashing egos, inflated ambitions, and the great shambles of the world trade system.* New York: PublicAffairs.

Hoekman, Bernard, and Michel Kostecki. 2010. *The political economy of the world trading system: From GATT to WTO.* 3rd ed. New York: Oxford University Press.

Jones, Kent. 2009. *Doha blues: Institutional crisis and reform in the WTO.* Oxford: Oxford University Press.

Robertson, David. 2000. Civil society and the WTO. *World Economy* 23(9): 1119–34.

Schott, Jeffrey J., ed. 2000. *The WTO after Seattle.* Washington, DC: Institute for International Economics.

After doing your general literature review, you may find that some assertions are not necessarily supported or that you want to study some of the questions raised. Robertson, for example, says that many NGOs involved in the protests in Seattle, Washington, had no obvious tie to any economic issues associated with the WTO, and he lists "teachers' unions, AIDS groups, church groups, animal rights groups, indigenous and women's groups" (2000, 1132). That is, Robertson argues that economic interests were not independent variables involved in promoting the protest. You may find other scholars who argue that economic interests are indeed important. You may want to see if this is true. If Robertson's assertion is not true, what were the economic issues associated with these groups? Of course, you will need to look at some other potential independent variables as well.

Sources for Choosing Cases and Gathering Information

http://www.wto.org/english/res_e/res_e.htm
> This is the resource page of the WTO.

http://depts.washington.edu/wtohist/index.htm
> The WTO History Project, a joint effort of several programs at the University of Washington, makes available a number of resources via this website.

http://www.globalexchange.org/wto/links.html
> Global Exchange gives information on opposition to the WTO.

http://www.law.duke.edu/lib/researchguides/gatt
> Duke University School of Law website with information on GATT/WTO.

Political Leaders

Political leaders are important to IPE because economic policies are inextricably linked to political processes. If you are interested in the politics involved, you may want to research what effects leaders' positions on particular international economic issues:

What factors affect leadership positions on (specific economic issue or policy)?

Areas of interest to you might include:

- Trade policy (including policies related to tariffs and trading agreements)
- Development policy (including the promotion of growth in economies worldwide)

In order to narrow your question to a reasonable project, you should read broadly on issues related to leaders and economic policymaking.

Resources on the International Economic Policymaking

Carbone, Maurizio. 2007. *The European Union and international development: The politics of foreign aid*. New York: Routledge.

Chorev, Nitsan. 2007. *Remaking U.S. trade policy: From protectionism to globalization*. Ithaca: Cornell University Press.

Skonieczny, Amy. 2001. Constructing NAFTA: Myth, representation, and the discursive construction of U.S. foreign policy. *International Studies Quarterly* 45(3): 433–54.

Spero, Joan and Jeffrey Hart. 2010. *The politics of international economic relations*. 7th ed. Boston: Wadsworth Cengage Learning.

You may choose to focus on the factors that affect how policy is made, but there are other interesting questions to ask that are related to political leaders and international economic policy. For example, you may study how leaders attempt to legitimize, or gain support for their preferred policies. For example, after reading Skonieczny's (2001) work, you might apply her method of analysis to understand the arguments used by political leaders to legitimize other international economic agreements. She argues that the discursive construction of NAFTA by political leaders led to public support for the agreement. You might want to test her hypothesis in different cases. If you pursue this research project, your question is:

Under what conditions does passage of a regional trade agreement become acceptable?

Here the focus is on how the agreement was described and explained, i.e. its discursive construction.

Resources on Agreements

http://tcc.export.gov/Trade_Agreements/All_Trade_Agreements/index.asp
The Trade Compliance Center (TCC), in the U.S. Department of Commerce's International Trade Administration, has a website with a listing of trade agreements.

http://www.wto.org/english/tratop_e/region_e/region_e.htm
WTO Regional trade agreements listing.

http://www.ustr.gov/trade-agreements
Office of the U.S. Trade Representative website for trade agreements.

THE ROLE OF PEOPLE IN DEVELOPMENT

Two major labels are used to describe complicated ongoing processes in international relations that involve both politics and economics: globalization and development. International relations textbooks discuss both of these concepts. Globalization can be defined as "the increasing integration of the world in terms of communications, culture, and economics" (Goldstein 2003, 547), and development can be defined as the process by which national income levels rise in a more complex and broader way that includes both social and economic changes. Globalization is covered in Chapter 9. The role of people in international development is addressed here.

One productive way to research the topic of development is to ask questions that address the complexities involved. First, make sure you understand the dynamics by reading some general information. Then, read more. You may want to start with the following resources.

Resources on Development

Barro, Robert J. 1997. *Determinants of economic growth: A cross-country empirical study.* Cambridge, MA: MIT Press.
Cypher, James M., and James L. Dietz. 2004. *The process of economic development.* 2nd ed. New York: Routledge.

Escobar, Arturo. 1995. *Encountering development: The making and unmaking of the third world*. Princeton, NJ: Princeton University Press.

Jameson, Kenneth P., and Charles K. Wilber, eds. 1996. *The political economy of development and underdevelopment*. 6th ed. New York: McGraw-Hill.

Kohli, Atul. 2004. *State-directed development: Political power and industrialization in the global periphery*. Cambridge: Cambridge University Press.

Mehrota, Santosh, and Richard Jolly, eds. 1997. *Development with a human face: Experiences in social achievement and economic growth*. New York: Oxford University Press.

Gender

As Nobel Prize winner Amartya Sen writes, "Nothing, arguably, is as important today in the political economy of development as an adequate recognition of political, economic and social participation and leadership of women" (1999, 203). You may have read about development and poverty, as well as the importance of women to economic development, improved health and welfare, and the alleviation of poverty. If not, you may want to learn more about this topic, which is a fascinating and important part of understanding development in the world today. There are a number of approaches to studying this area. Data are more accessible now than in the recent past, and international organizations are paying attention to this important issue. First, learn more about the role of gender in economic development. If your textbook does not contain much information, do not be deterred. You can begin your reading with some of the resources listed here.

Resources on Gender

http://www.genderanddevelopment.org/
Website for the journal *Gender and Development,* which contains articles on this topic.

Beneria, Lourdes. 2003. *Gender, development, and globalization: Economics as if all people mattered*. New York: Routledge.

Duncan, W. Raymond, Barbara Jancar-Webster, and Bob Switky. 2003. *World politics in the twenty-first century*. New York: Longman. [See especially Chapter 10, "Women, poverty and human rights."]

Massiah, Joycelin, ed. 1992. *Women in developing economies: Making visible the invisible*. New York: Berg.

Momsen, Janet Henshall. 2004. *Gender and development*. London: Routledge.

Nussbaum, Martha C. 2000. *Women and human development: The capabilities approach*. Cambridge: Cambridge University Press. [See especially pp. 290–97.]

Parpart, Jane L. 2000. Rethinking participation, empowerment, and development from a gender perspective. In *Transforming development: Foreign aid for a changing world*, ed. Jim Freedman. Toronto: University of Toronto Press.

Scott, Catherine V. 1996. *Gender and development: Rethinking modernization and dependency theory.* Boulder, CO: Lynne Rienner.

Sen, Amartya. 1999. *Development as freedom.* New York: Alfred A. Knopf. [See especially Chapter 8, "Women's agency and social change."]

There are a number of ways to study the role of women in economic development. One way is to look at under what conditions particular development programs or plans are supported and/or implemented. It is generally accepted now, for example, that female literacy is an effective way to combat population growth. Population growth is, of course, a problem in much of the world. You might study under what conditions political leaders promote, accept, and/or adopt programs that encourage female literacy:

Under what conditions do [countries/regions/communities] adopt literacy programs for women?

In particular, you might look at the role of external and internal independent variables to see if there are patterns across cases. External factors may include the presence of development workers representing IGOs or NGOs. Internal factors may include policy entrepreneurs or leaders who champion such programs.

Sources for Choosing Cases and Gathering Information

http://genderstats.worldbank.org
   This World Bank site offers statistics on gender and development.

http://www.worldbank.org/gender/relatedlinks/related.htm
   Gender Net is a World Bank site that contains links to other sites on women and development.

http://hdr.undp.org/reports
   The United Nations Development Programme (UNDP) commissions and posts the Human Development Report annually.

http://www.undp.org/women/
   The UNDP website on women's empowerment.

http://www.ncrw.org/issues-expertise
   The National Council for Research on Women's site contains links to global information.

Corruption

Another way to study the role of individuals in economic development is to look at the role of corruption in the process of development. There is a debate among some scholars about this role with one group of scholars arguing that corruption hurts economic development whereas another group's research suggests that some level of corruption "greases the wheels" of economic development. You will need to read about corruption and development to get some background on this.

Resources on Corruption and Development

Aidt, Toke S. 2009. Corruption, institutions, and economic development. *Oxford Review of Economic Policy* 25(2): 271–91.

Egger, Peter and Hans Winner. 2005. Evidence on corruption as an incentive for foreign direct investment. *European Journal of Political Economy* 21: 932–52.

Fisman, Raymond and Edwar Miguel. 2010. *Economic gangsters: Corruption, violence, and the poverty of nations.* Princeton: Princeton University Press.

Leff, Nathaniel. 1964. Economic development through bureaucratic corruption. *American Behavioral Scientist* 8(3): 8–14.

Rose-Ackerman, Susan. 1999. *Corruption and government: Causes, consequences and reform.* Cambridge: Cambridge University Press.

Smith, B.C. 2007. *Good governance and economic development.* London: Palgrave.

Treisman, Daniel. 2007. What have we learned about the causes of corruption from ten years of cross-national empirical research? *Annual Review of Political Science* 10: 211–44.

After reading about the relationship between corruption and development, you can set out a research question:

Under what conditions does political corruption affect economic development?

To answer this question you would first need to develop a list of countries that have low, medium, and high levels of political corruption and low, medium, and high levels of economic development. One measure of corruption levels can be found at

- http://corruptionresearchnetwork.org/datasets (Transparency International)

Triesman (2007, 241) shows that "countries are perceived to be more corrupt if they depend on fuel exports, have intrusive business regulations, and suffer from unpredictable inflation." You may want to analyze these factors in a few case studies.

GENERAL DATA SOURCES FOR CHOOSING CASES AND GATHERING EVIDENCE

The following sources will help you gather information on global economics.

http://www.wto.org/english/res_e/statis_e/statis_e.htm
General statistics are available at this WTO site.

http://globaledge.msu.edu/ibrd/busresmain.asp?ResourceCategoryID=10
Michigan State University's site has a huge number of links to information on global economics.

International Organization and Law

In addition to international conflict, U.S. foreign policy, and international political economy a fourth major area of study in international relations is international organization and international law. Scholars of international organization study how states and other international actors organize their interactions. They often focus on international organizations and international law or, in other words, the organizational structures and rules of the system. Your textbook probably talks quite a bit about the importance of international organizations in IR and may emphasize the role of the United Nations (UN), for example. International law also plays a role as states often agree that treaties, custom, principles, and legal scholarship can shape or guide interactions between or among states.

If you are interested in international organization, you can approach the topic in a number of ways. In this chapter, we highlight two options. You can focus on a particular issue, such as the environment, human rights, or war crimes, or you can focus on a particular actor within the international system, including international governmental organizations, nongovernmental organizations, and multinational corporations. Of course, these two approaches can be tied together. Here, however, we separate the two areas in order to develop some initial research questions you might address.

ISSUE AREAS

One interesting way to study international organization is to look at different issues of importance to the international community and the conditions that affect cooperation in those areas. Then, your general research topic is:

What factors affect international cooperation in [issue area]?

For example, research about the environment and human rights falls into this category. One way to study cooperation in a particular issue area is to study the role of norms and regimes in that cooperation. Norms are "shared expectations about what behavior is considered proper" (Goldstein 2008, 49–50), and international regimes are "a set of rules, norms, and procedures around which the expectations of actors converge in a certain international issue area" (Goldstein 2008, 87). After you reread what your textbook has to say, you may want to start your general literature review with some of the works cited here.

Resources on Norms and Regimes

Betsill, Michele M., Kathryn Hochstetler, and Dimitris Stevis, eds. 2006. *International environmental politics*. New York: Palgrave MacMillan.

Finnemore, Martha, and Kathryn Sikkink. 1998. International norm dynamics and political change. *International Organization* 52(4): 887–917.

Hasenclever, Andreas, Peter Mayer, and Volker Rittberger. 1997. *Theories of international regimes*. New York: Cambridge University Press.

Krasner, Stephen D., ed. 1983. *International regimes*. Ithaca, NY: Cornell University Press.

Kratochwil, Friedrich W. 1989. *Rules, norms, and decisions: On the conditions of practical and legal reasoning in international relations and domestic affairs*. New York: Cambridge University Press.

McElroy, Robert. 1993. *Morality and American foreign policy*. Princeton, NJ: Princeton University Press.

Towns, Ann E. 2010. *Women and states: Norms and hierarchies in international society*. Cambridge: Cambridge University Press.

Environmental Treaties

One of the major topics addressed by international relations scholars is the strategies that states use to overcome problems of collective goods under certain conditions. Collective goods are those goods available to everyone in a group regardless of their contribution. The problem comes when too many actors lower or withdraw their contribution and the goods are not created or are lost. The classic example is the environment. If too many states do not abide by environmental agreements, environmental degradation may affect the whole world. If you are interested in this, you might ask the question:

What factors contribute to agreement on international environmental treaties?

After reading your textbook, you should conduct a literature review. Some scholarly works on the environment are listed here.

Resources on the Environment

Axelrod, Regina S., David L. Downie, and Norman J. Vig., eds. 2005. *The global environment: Institutions, law, and policy* 2nd ed. Washington, DC: Congressional Quarterly Press. [See especially, the chapter by David Leonard Downie, titled "Global environmental governance through regimes" and Michael Faure and Jurgen Lefevere's Chapter 9, pp. 163–80, "Compliance with global environmental policy"]

Hempel, Lamont C. 1996. *Environmental governance: The global challenge*. Washington, DC: Island Press. [See especially Chapter 5, "The environmental policy-making process."]

Keohane, Robert O., Marc A. Levy, and Peter M. Haas. 1993. *Institutions for the earth: Sources of effective international environmental protection*. Cambridge, MA: MIT Press.

Victor, David G., Kal Raustiala, and Eugene B. Skolnikoff. 1998. *The implementation and effectiveness of international environmental commitments: Theory and practice*. Cambridge, MA: MIT Press.

Young, Oran R., ed. 1994. *International governance: Protecting the environment in a stateless society*. Ithaca, NY: Cornell University Press.

————. 1999. *The effectiveness of international environmental regimes: Causal connections and behavioral mechanisms*. Cambridge, MA: MIT Press.

After reading about international environmental agreements, you will need to pick a case or cases and develop hypotheses. You will set out the independent variables that you will analyze across your cases. For example, Victor, Raustiala, and Skolnikoff (1998) identify the following independent variables: (1) the nature of the problem at hand, (2) configurations of power, (3) institutions, (4) the nature of commitments, (5) linkages with other issues and objectives, (6) exogenous factors, and (7) public concern. You may look at the role of a number of these independent variables across cases or look at a number of these factors in one case. Remember that you will have to explain how you will measure (or operationalize) the factors you decide to include in your conceptual analysis.

Sources for Choosing Cases and Gathering Information

http://www.unep.org/
   This UN Environment Programme site gives information on the work of the UN in the area of environment and development. This site will provide both general and specific information related to the environment and for gathering evidence on your dependent and independent variables.

http://fletcher.tufts.edu/multilaterals/
   The Fletcher School of International Diplomacy makes available the texts of international multilateral conventions and other international legal instruments in an easily accessible database organized by subject. In addition to a general subject heading associated with the environment,

the database also sections out treaties on atmosphere and space, biodiversity, and marine and coastal protection.

http://www.nyulawglobal.org/globalex/International_Environmental_
Legal_Research.htm

GlobaLex is a website designed to facilitate high-level research on international, foreign, and comparative law. Their guide to international environmental legal research is an exceptional resource for finding definitions of key terms and as a portal to other resources valuable for collecting information on environmental treaties. Once you have picked a treaty or set of treaties to focus upon for your study, this website can assist you in specific information regarding your cases.

Barry, John, and Gene Frankland. 2002. *International encyclopedia of environmental politics*. London: Routledge.

Human Rights

Many students are interested in human rights in the international system. One way to study this issue area is to look at how different states implement human rights:

What accounts for differences in the implementation of human rights norms?

First, you should review what your textbook has to say about human rights. If you would like additional general information on human rights, the UN provides a useful research guide that can be found at: http://www.un.org/Depts/dhl/resguide/spechr.htm. After establishing your general foundation of knowledge, you can begin your broad literature review with the following resources.

Resources on Human Rights

Human Rights and/or International Norms

Risse, Thomas, Stephen C. Ropp, and Kathryn Sikkink, eds. 1999. *The power of human rights: International norms and domestic change*. New York: Cambridge University Press.

Sikkink, Kathryn. 1993. Human rights, principled issue-networks, and sovereignty in Latin America. *International Organization* 47: 411–41.

Wendt, Alexander. 1992. Anarchy is what states make of it: The social construction of power politics. *International Organization* 46(2): 391–425.

More General Resources on Human Rights

Donnelly, Jack. 2006. *International human rights*. Boulder, CO: Westview Press.

Forsythe, David. 2006. *The internationalization of human rights*, 2nd ed. Washington, DC: Lexington Books.

Gillies, David. 1996. *Between principle and practice: Human rights in North–South relations*. Montreal: McGill-Queen's University Press.

Ishay, Micheline R. 2008. *The history of human rights: From ancient times to the globalization era*. Berkeley: University of California Press.

Perry, Michael. 1998. *The idea of human rights: Four inquiries*. New York: Oxford University Press.

After you have done your literature review, you will choose independent variables, select a case or cases, and develop hypotheses. First, you should be clear about what you mean in your question by "implementation of human rights norms." Risse, Ropp, and Sikkink, for example, argue that five phases characterize the implementation of human rights norms in different countries: (1) repression and activation of network, (2) denial, (3) tactical concessions, (4) "prescriptive status," and (5) rule-consistent behavior (1999, 22–35). You will need to understand how these phases were identified systematically across a number of cases. You can then select cases in a number of different ways, including the following:

- Choose cases where implementation falls into the same category (e.g., denial).
- Choose cases of different phases of implementation.

What independent variables might help to explain the similarities or differences? Focus on these in your research.

Sources for Choosing Cases and Gathering Information

http://www.lib.umich.edu/govdocs/forcoun.html#human
> This University of Michigan site contains a whole section of human rights links, including links to Amnesty International, the U.S. State Department, and a large number of other resources for the study of human rights.

http://ciri.binghamton.edu/
> The Cingranelli-Richards (CIRI) Human Rights Dataset contains information on government respect for fifteen internationally recognized human rights for 195 countries, annually from 1981–2007.

http://www.bayefsky.com
> This website was developed by Professor A.F. Bayefsky of York University, Toronto, Canada. This website serves as a Portal to UN human rights treaty information and also provides texts of treaties and specific information on how global human rights treaties are implemented. Information is categorized by state, subject matter, and category. This website will be valuable for dependent and independent variable information.

http://www.unhchr.ch/tbs/doc.nsf
> The UN database on human rights treaties.

http://www.state.gov/www/global/human_rights/hrp_reports_mainhp.html
Annual state department reports that review the human rights practices in foreign countries. Reports are available online from 1993
forward.

War Crimes

Another area of interest for many students is that of international law and the
conduct of war. Topics here include war crimes, the designation and treatment
of prisoners of war, and what constitutes a just war. If, for example, you are
interested in war crimes, you might ask this question:

What factors affect the prosecution of individuals for war crimes?

First, you will need to read about the underlying issues, principles,
and history.

Resources on War Crimes

Byers, Michael. 2005. *War law: Understanding international law and
armed conflict*. Berkeley, CA: Grove Press.
Falk, Richard, Irene Gendzier, and Robert Jay Lifton. 2006. *Crimes of
war: Iraq*. New York: Nation Books.
Howard, Michael. 1997. *The laws of war: Constraints on warfare in the
western world*. New Haven, CT: Yale University Press.
Meernik, James. 2003. Victor's justice or the law? Judging and punishing
at the International Criminal Tribunal for the former Yugoslavia.
Journal of Conflict Resolution 47(2): 140–62.

After reading the piece by Meernik (2003), perhaps you will be interested
in whether his findings about Yugoslavia apply across other cases. His research shows that punishment of those tried for war crimes was, for the most
part, based on the seriousness of the crimes. This disputes those who argue
that punishment is politically motivated. You could develop a study that looks
at specific cases across different conflicts and across time periods.

Sources for Choosing Cases and Gathering Information

http://www.ess.uwe.ac.uk/genocide/
Dr. Stuart D. Stein's website covers resources on genocide, war crimes,
and mass killing.

http://www.un.org/icty/
This UN website discusses the International Criminal Tribunal for the
former Yugoslavia.

http://www1.umn.edu/humanrts/instree/auox.htm
This is the University of Minnesota's Human Rights Library website on
war crimes, crimes against humanity, genocide, and terrorism.

ACTORS

Another way to study international cooperation, broadly understood, is to study how international actors act and under what circumstances they choose to either cooperate or not. Your textbook may place the most emphasis on states as actors in the international system; however, it will surely mention a number of other actors as well. International governmental organizations (IGOs), nongovernmental organizations (NGOs), quasi-nongovernmental organizations (QUANGOs; NGOs that receive most of their resources from governments), donor-organized NGOs (DONGOs; NGOs that receive most funding from particular donors), and multinational corporations (MNCs) are international actors that may be of interest to you. You may want to research the conditions under which these different types of international organizations behave differently or similarly. You may be interested in one particular international organization. For example, you could focus your research on the UN, an important international organization covered by almost every international relations textbook. You may also be interested in international courts, another example of an international organization. Remember that you will narrow your topic considerably once you have chosen your general area of interest.

Joining International Governmental Organizations

Many textbooks explain that the rise in the number of international organizations is due to a growing interdependence among states in an increasingly globalized political world. You may want to explore this question a bit further in a research paper of your own:

Under what conditions do states join international governmental organizations?

First you will need to reread your textbook and understand what it says about international organizations in general. Then you should read more, perhaps beginning with the sources listed here. Remember, however, that this list provides only a starting point for a more general literature review.

Resources on International Organizations

Finnemore, Martha. 1996. *National interests in international society.* Ithaca, NY: Cornell University Press.

Hawkins, Darren G. 2006. *Delegation and agency in international organizations.* Cambridge: Cambridge University Press.

Karns, Margaret P. and Karen A. Mingst. 2009. *International organizations: The politics and processes of global governance.* Boulder, CO: Lynne Rienner Publishers.

Keohane, Robert O. 1998. International institutions: Can interdependence work? *Foreign Policy* 110: 82–96.

After conducting a literature review, you will choose independent variables and a case or cases and then set out hypotheses. One way to approach the initial question about the conditions under which states join IGOs involves choosing to focus on one particular IGO and assessing whether or not particular independent variables were important. Finnemore (1996) looks at this when writing about new state bureaucracies, but you might want to apply her framework to international organizations. She discusses the following points.

- Specific issues: States join because the new organization addresses a particular issue of importance to the state.
- Development or modernization: As states develop, they require different organizations to handle new problems or issues brought about by technological or economic changes associated with development.
- Security: Military or security concerns prompt membership in the organization.
- Supply-driven explanations: States join international organizations because of ideas from outside the state about what is right or proper. These ideas can be fostered by (1) individuals, (2) international organizations, (3) NGOs, and (4) other states.

To do this type of analysis, you could choose an international organization and study why particular countries join, or you could choose a country and analyze why it does or does not join a number of international organizations.

Source for Choosing Cases and Gathering Information

http://www.lib.umich.edu/govdocs/intl.html

The University of Michigan maintains an excellent site that contains alphabetical links to a large number of IGOs and NGOs. Several links to UN sites are included.

States as UN Members

Another way to look at international organizations is to study how states behave as members. There are a number of different potential explanations for why states behave the way they do within international organizations, and you may want to look at these. Suppose, for example, that you are interested in the factors that affect states' behaviors in the UN. You might ask this question:

What accounts for the voting pattern of a state (or states) in the UN Security Council?

If you were to pursue this question, you would begin with a review of the UN structure discussed in your textbook. Then you would turn to a general review of the literature on the UN (including the Security Council). Some starting points are listed here.

Resources on the UN

Hanhimaki, Jussi M. 2008. *The United Nations: A very short introduction.* Oxford: Oxford University Press.

Sutterlin, James. 2003. *The United Nations and the maintenance of international security: A challenge to be met.* Westport, CT: Praeger.

Voeten, Erik. 2001. Outside options and the logic of Security Council action. *The American Political Science Review* 95: 845–58.

Weiss, Thomas G., David P. Forsythe, and Roger A. Coate. 2007. *The United Nations and changing world politics,* 5th ed. Boulder, CO: Westview.

Ziring, Lawrence, Robert E. Riggs, and Jack C. Plano. 2005. *The United Nations: International organization and world politics,* 4th ed. Belmont, CA: Wadsworth Publishing.

After reading about the UN, you will be able to choose independent variables and case(s) and develop hypotheses. What is interesting about this question is that it combines foreign policy issues with the role of international organizations. One way to approach this question would be to compare two or more countries. Another option is to focus on one state. For example, Voeten (2001) argues that China abstains to express disagreement with a particular Security Council action or resolution only when the United States has viable options for pursuing that action outside of the UN. You may want to study the history of Chinese abstentions. You may find that other independent variables are involved, or you may find that the evidence supports Voeten's assertion.

Sources for Choosing Cases and Gathering Information

http://www.un.org/documents/scres.htm

You can access Security Council resolutions by year through this UN site. Make sure to get the number of the resolution if you are planning to search for the voting record.

http://unbisnet.un.org

This UN page allows you to search for voting records. You must know the Security Council resolution number or topic to search. (You cannot, for example, search for all votes by China, except individually by number or topic.)

Osmanczyk, Edmund. 2003. *Encyclopedia of the United Nations and international agreements.* New York: Routledge. This reference book covers the UN and international agreements.

International Courts as an International Actor

For those interested in international law and the bodies that are involved in the development of international legal frameworks, a final area of research could be international organizations such as the World Court (formally called the International Court of Justice—ICJ), the International Criminal Court (ICC), or regional organizations such as the European Court of Justice or the African Court of Human and Peoples' Rights.

Resources on International Courts

For differences between the ICJ and ICC, see:
http://www.insidejustice.com/law/index.php/intl/2008/11/10/
    differences_icc_icj
Arnull, Anthony. 2006. *The European Union and its Court of Justice*, 2nd ed. Oxford: Oxford University Press.
Lowe, Vaughan and Malgosia Fitsmaurice. 2007. *Fifty years of the International Court of Justice: Essays in Honour of Sir Robert Jennings*. Cambridge: Cambridge University Press.
Schiff, Benjamin. 2008. *Building the International Criminal Court*. Cambridge: Cambridge University Press.
Simmons, Beth and Allison Danner. 2010. Credible commitments and the International Criminal Court. *International Organization*. 64: 225–56.

After reading about the various international courts, you must narrow your research topic. You may, for example, study a relationship among different variables or factors that other scholars have discussed in their work. For instance, Simmons and Danner pose an interesting question: Why do states agree to join the International Criminal Court? Put another way, the question becomes:

What factors affect why states join the International Criminal Court?

Simmons and Danner find that "the states that are both the least and the most vulnerable to the possibility of an ICC case affecting their citizens have committed most readily to the ICC, while potentially vulnerable states with credible alternative means to hold leaders accountable do not." You may choose to study particular cases that either do or do not follow this pattern. Your contribution will be explaining the factors that affect a state's decision to join the ICC.

Sources for Choosing Cases and Gathering Information

http://www9.georgetown.edu/faculty/ev42/ICdata.htm
    Georgetown's site on international courts data.

http://www.pict-pcti.org/index.html
    Project on International Tribunals and Courts contains information on a range of international courts and tribunals. Click on courts and tribunals to get information on specific entities, such as:

http://www.pict-pcti.org/courts/ACHPR.html
    African Court of Human and Peoples' Rights.

http://www.icj-cij.org/
International Court of Justice site.

http://www.icc-cpi.int/Menus/ICC?lan=en-GB
International Criminal Court site.

http://www.echr.coe.int/echr/Homepage_EN
Council of Europe site that contains information on the European Court of Human Rights.

GENERAL DATA SOURCES FOR CHOOSING CASES AND GATHERING EVIDENCE

The following sources will help you gather information on international organizations.

http://www.library.northwestern.edu/govinfo/resource/internat/igo.html
Northwestern University has developed a website that contains an index to international governmental organizations.

http://www.uia.org/statistics/pub.php
The Union of International Associations maintains a website that contains statistics on international organizations and meetings.

http://library.duke.edu/research/subject/guides/ngo_guide/
Duke University has an online resource guide to nongovernmental organizations.

http://www.icrc.org/web/eng/siteeng0.nsf/iwpList2/Info_resources:
IHL_databases
The International Committee of the Red Cross has a website that contains two databases of international humanitarian law. One database contains treaties, and the other covers implementation.

Globalization/ Global Issues

A n increasingly important area for study within international relations is globalization. Globalization addresses the effects of increasing integration in communications, culture, and economics. A revolution in communication and transportation technologies has increased the interaction of people around the world and this has important repercussions for international politics. Knowledge of events happening on the other side of the planet is shared via international news and the Internet; people travel across state borders with important implications for security and health; and people struggle to make sense of place and identity in an increasingly globalized world. In this chapter, we discuss three important areas associated with globalization:

- movement of information
- movement of people
- effects on identity

Globalization can be defined as "the increasing integration of the world in terms of communications, culture, and economics" (Goldstein 2003, 547) and is often said to encourage commonalities among individuals (the McWorld syndrome) and emphasize differences (including national differences). Most scholars recognize that this is much more complicated than an either-or process. One productive way to research these issues is to ask questions that address the complexities involved. First, make sure you understand the dynamics by reading some general information. Then, read more. You may want to start with the following resources.

RESOURCES ON GLOBALIZATION

General Resources on Globalization

Bhagwati, Jagdish. 2004. *In defense of globalization*. New York: Oxford University Press.

113

Brysk, Alison. 2002. *Globalization and human rights*. Berkeley: University of California Press.

Held, David. 2002. *Globalization/anti-globalization*. Cambridge, UK: Polity Press.

Mott, William. 2004. *Globalization: People, perspectives, and progress*. Westport, CT: Praeger.

Nye, Joseph. 2004. *Power in the global information age: From realism to globalization*. London: Routledge.

Stiglitz, Joseph E. 2006. *Making globalization work*. New York: W. W. Norton & Co.

MOVEMENT OF INFORMATION: INTERNATIONAL COMMUNICATION AND MEDIA

Within the last one hundred years or so a communication technology revolution has changed how information flows in the international system and this has important repercussions for how people, groups, and states interact. Mass media and the computer have increased the speed and reach of communication and now news and information can be shared among a greater number of people. Changes in international communication have changed the way groups and people in the world share ideas and organize. There are two ways you may want to study changes associated with the movement of information. One is through the study of policies related to communication technologies and the other is through how international groups use communication technologies and information.

First you will need an overview of how scholars have studied the information revolution and international politics.

Resources on International Communication

Conway, Maura. 2007 *Terrorism, the Internet, and international relations: The governance conundrum*. In *Power and security in the information age: Investigating the role of the state in cyberspace*, eds. Myriam Dunn Cavelty, Victor Mauer, Krishna-Hensel, and Sai Felicia, 95–127. Ashgate.

Deibert, Ronald J., John G. Palfrey, Rafal Rohozinski, and Jonathan Zittrain, eds. 2010 *Access controlled: The shaping of power, rights and rule in cyberspace*. Cambridge: MIT Press.

Hanson, Elizabeth C. 2008. *The information revolution and world politics*. Lanham, MD: Rowman & Littlefield.

Mueller, Milton. 2010. Networks and States: *The global politics of internet governance*. Cambridge: MIT Press.

Wilson, Ernest J. 2006. *The information revolution and developing countries*. Cambridge: MIT Press.

Internet Policies

One area of research that may be of interest to you is the study of the role of the Internet in international politics. Some suggest that the Internet can facilitate sharing across international borders and this may present political problems for states. Political leaders may try to control the flow of information from outside state borders and you may be interested in this. Hanson, for example, suggests that the Internet and other information technologies can affect the power of state leaders. Thus, one research questions that is important is:

What factors affect state Internet policies?

To address this question you may want to focus on cases within one country or across a small number of countries in which state political leaders have intervened to shape Internet policies. China is one country that has set out controls for the Internet, but other countries have done so as well. You may want to study under what conditions states perceive action in this area to be particularly important. You will need to gather information on Chinese policies on the Internet. A brief list follows.

Resources on International Policy and China

Qiang, Christine Zhen–Wei. 2007. *China's information revolution: Managing the economic and social transformation.* World Bank Publications.

Zheng, Yongian, and Guoguang Wu. 2005. Information technology, public sphere, and collective action in China. *Comparative Political Studies.* 38(5): 507–36.

Zhu, Xufeng. 2008. Strategy of Chinese policy entrepreneurs in the third sector: Challenges of "Technical Infeasibility." *Policy Sciences* 41(4): 315–34.

Once you have read the work of other scholars, you can design a research project that addresses Chinese Internet policy in a new way. Remember as discussed in Chapter 3, this could mean looking at a new case, timeframe, specific policy, or it could mean studying a new group of independent variables in a previously explored case. Below are some places to look when developing your project.

Sources for Choosing Cases and Gathering Information

http://news.bbc.co.uk/2/hi/asia-pacific/8460129.stm
   BBC: Timeline of China and net censorship.

http://cyber.law.harvard.edu/research/surveillance
   Berkman Center for Internet and Society, Harvard University.

http://opennet.net/
   Open Net initiative: "ONI's mission is to identify and document Internet filtering and surveillance, and to promote and inform wider public dialogs about such practices."

Transnational Advocacy

The rapid movement and accessibility of information may affect how groups form, organize, and participate in the international system. This includes groups called transnational advocacy groups, a type of nongovernmental organization (NGO). If access to the Internet is available, potential members of these groups are not constrained by state borders or the difficulty and expense of travel. Hanson suggests a number of different ways that you might study the role of information and transnational advocacy organizations. For example, you might ask:

What factors affect communication strategies of transnational actors?

First you will need to understand something about transnational advocacy networks more generally. The following resources may be of help.

Resources on Transnational Advocacy Networks

Bennett, W. Lance. 2003. New media power: The Internet and global activism. In *Contesting media power.*, eds. Nick Couldry and James Curran, 17–37. Lanham, MD: Rowman & Littlefield.

————. 2005. Social movements beyond borders: Understanding two eras of transnational activism. In *Transnational protest and global activism*, eds. Donatella Della Porta and Sidney Tarrow. Lanham, MD: Rowman & Littlefield.

de Jong, Wilma, Martin Shaw, and Neil Stammers, eds. 2005. *Global activism, global media.* Ann Arbor: Pluto Press.

Keck, Margaret and Kathryn Sikkink. 1998. *Activists beyond borders: Advocacy networks in international politics.* Ithaca: Cornell University Press.

Tarrow, Sidney. 2005. *The new transnational activism.* NY: Cambridge University Press.

Once you have read broadly about transnational advocacy organizations, you will see that many scholars argue that organizational structure and technological capabilities affect the communication strategies of these organizations. You may want to do a research project that looks at these relationships. To do this you will have to choose cases and there are a number of ways to do this. You may compare organizations with different structures, for example. Another way to organize the research would be to look at communication strategies of one organization across different issue areas, over time, under different leaders, or in response to different types of events.

Sources for Choosing Cases and Gathering Information

http://library.duke.edu/research/subject/guides/ngo_guide/ngo_links/a-e.html
Duke University's listing of NGOs.

http://library.duke.edu/research/subject/guides/ngo_guide/ngo_links/
transnational.html
Duke University's listing of transnational organizations, including
subject and affiliation.

MOVEMENT OF PEOPLE

The study of globalization also includes the study of the movement of people.
State and international policies and developments in transportation technologies such as the airplane have increased the movement of people around the
world and this has important implications for international politics. Two important areas of research related to the movement of people are migration and
health. Migration, whether due to conflict economic pressures or other issues,
has important effects on international politics.

Migration

There are a number of important areas to study if you are interested in migration. You may be interested in

- state policies about immigration or immigrants,
- the experience of those who are immigrants or refugees,
- how international politics affects migration, or
- international responses to humanitarian and other issues associated with
  migration or refugees.

A broad question that you can use to begin a research project could be:

What factors best explain population movements in particular regions of the world?

Case selection will be very important with this type of question.
You should first review your textbook for what is generally understood
about population migration and refugee migration patterns. Second,
review the types of projects we address in Chapter 3. Then we
recommend that you look at the migration or refugee data for
population movements that *do not* fit with readily understandable
patterns of activity. In other words, look for anomalies within the data.

Resources on Migration

International Migration Review—Scholarly Journal.
Castles, Stephen, Mark J. Miller, and Giuseppe Ammendola. 2003. *The
age of migration: International population movements in the modern
world*. NY: The Guilford Press.
Dauvergne, Catherine. 2008. *Making people illegal: What globalization
means for migration and law*. Cambrige: Cambridge University Press.

Koser, Khalid. 2007. *International migration: A very short history*. Oxford: Oxford University Press.

Mahler, Sarah J., and Patricia R. Pessar. 2006. Gender matters: Ethnographers bring gender from the periphery toward the core of migration studies. *International Migration Review* 40(1): 27–63.

For a more general question on migration you could take the following approach:

Under what conditions are states most likely to adopt policies that restrict the free movement of populations?

This type of question can be interpreted to be about the factors that lead states to adopt rigid border protection policies. This may take you into the literature on conflict, health, or even international security. Therefore, case selection and time frame will be very important. Remember, *while case selection is subjective, it should never be arbitrary*. We again suggest that you refer to Chapter 3 for ways to choose cases.

Sources for Choosing Cases and Gathering Information

http://stats.oecd.org/Index.aspx?datasetcode=MIG
    Organization for Economic Cooperation and Development data.

http://www.migrationinformation.org/DataHub/
    Migration Policy Institute data hub.

http://www.unhcr.org/pages/49c3646c4d6.html
    United Nations Refugee Agency's site.

Health

Another important area associated with the movement of people in the world is in the area of health. Many students are interested in the study of how globalization affects issues related to the health of individuals in countries around the world. For example, many are concerned about how AIDS and other infectious diseases affect millions around the world. In addition, due to increased travel and movement, diseases can spread rapidly as people move from place to place. One example of this is the fear associated with the spread of the H1N1 virus in 2009–2010. You may be interested in how states coordinate responses to something like the H1N1 virus. In addition, you may be interested in broader issues associated with human health and international relations.

The following research topics may help guide you:

- what factors affect how international organizations coordinate responses to health crises
- what factors affect the role of private businesses, including the pharmaceutical industry, in international health issues
- under what conditions diseases affect a state's security

First, you will have read more broadly about international health issues.

Resources on International Health

Cooper, Andrew F. and John J. Kirton. 2009. *Innovation in global health governance*. Ashgate.

Gunn, William A., P. B. Mansourian, Piel, Anthony, A. Michael Davies, and Bruce Sayers. 2010. *Understanding the global dimensions of health*. Springer.

Koehn, Peter H. Globalization, 2006. Migration health, and educational preparation for transnational medical encounters. *Globalization and Health* 2(2).

MacLean, Sandra J., Pieter Fourie, and Sherri Brown, eds. 2009. *Health for some: The political economy of global health governance*. NY: Palgrave.

An initial project question associated with a world health concern could be:

What factors best explain differences in the international response to recognized transnational epidemics?

What students should be wary of doing when setting up a project on health issues, is to avoid developing a question that is an epidemiological project study rather than an international relations project study. Project design will be most successful if the project question concentrates on policy and state responses to health problems rather than the root cause of disease itself.

Sources for Choosing Cases and Gathering Information

http://www.aber.ac.uk/interpol/en/research/CHAIR/chair.html
Aberystwyth University's Centre for Health and International Relations.

http://www.hopkinsglobalhealth.org/resources/
Johns Hopkins Center for Global Health.

http://www.unaids.org/en/default.asp
UNAIDS: The Joint United Nations on HIV/AIDS.

http://www.who.int/en/
The World Health Organization site contains information on health and specific countries.

http://www.cartercenter.org/health/index.html
The Carter Center's health programs.

EFFECTS OF GLOBALIZATION

A final area of research discussed here is the effects of globalization. You will not be able to do research on the effects of globalization on individuals, but you will be able to study issues related to national and international identity and culture. One important area of study related to globalization involves how people understand their place in the increasingly interconnected and globalized world. To what degree do people become more cosmopolitan or "global" in outlook and identification, and to what degree do people cherish and seek to reinforce local or national identities, culture, and language?

National Identity

One of the arguments about globalization, and particularly about economic liberalism, is that it diminishes differences between or among people, and this may include the loss of national differences or identity. Others argue that this is a complicated process and that both people and leaders have maintained national identity in a number of different ways. You may be interested in looking at this dynamic by studying the actions of leaders who reinforce national identity even as they make agreements enhancing economic interdependence. One question would be this:

As interdependence increases, under what conditions and how do political leaders reinforce national identity?

If you are interested in this topic, first reread what a textbook has to say about globalization *and* nationalism. Then you need to focus on the more specific scholarly literature. A few resources are listed here.

Resources on National Identity

Biersteker, T. J., and C. Weber, eds. 1996. *State sovereignty as social construct*. Cambridge, UK: Cambridge University Press.

Cha, Victor D. 2000. Globalization and the study of international security. *Journal of Peace Research* 37(3): 391–403.

Goff, Patricia. 2000. Invisible borders: Economic liberalization and national identity. *International Studies Quarterly* 44(4): 533–63.

After your general literature review, you must choose a case or cases and develop hypotheses around a limited number of independent variables. You could approach this in a number of different ways. For example, you could analyze an economic agreement and study how leaders legitimize or explain this agreement to citizens. Is nationalism taken into account, at least in rhetoric? If so, under what conditions? Another way is to look, as Goff (2000) does, at the entire context of the economic agreement to see whether important national characteristics are protected or included in the agreement. Here you would have to choose an economic agreement or set of agreements as case studies. It may be interesting to look at the conditions under which individual states try to protect national or cultural characteristics or identity and when they do not.

Source for Choosing Cases and Gathering Information

http://www.fletcher.tufts.edu/multilaterals.html

Tufts University maintains a site with links to treaties and research strategies.

Culture—UNESCO Sites

Another way to study the effects of globalization is to study how people understand and structure history and culture. For example, while globalization may allow people to learn about other cultures and peoples, there is a strong countervailing pressure to protect national and ethnic culture, language, history, and identity. One interesting area to study would be to look at how international organizations address issues related to culture and history. First you will have to read broadly about these issues.

Resources on Historical Sites and Culture in a Global World

International Journal of Heritage Studies

Ashworth, G.J., and Tunbridge, J.E. 1999. Old cities, new pasts: Heritage planning in selected cities of Central Europe, *GeoJournal* 49: 105–116.

Hall, C.M. 2001. World heritage and tourism. *Tourism Recreation Research* 26(1): 1–3.

Chape, Stuart, Mark Spalding, and Martin Jenkins. 2008. *The world's protected areas: Status, values and prospects in the 21st century.* Univ de Castilla La Mancha.

Ryan, Jason and Sari Silvanto. 2009. The World Heritage List: The making and management of a brand. *Place Branding and Public Diplomacy* 5(4): 290–300.

Once you have read about historical sites and culture, you may want to narrow your research project by looking at the United Nations Educational, Scientific and Cultural Organization (UNESCO). UNESCO's mission is to foster "cultural diversity, intercultural dialogue, and a culture of peace." You may be interested in this mission and want to explore it further. First, explore the UNESCO website (http://www.unesco.org/new/en/unesco/about-us/who-we-are/introducing-unesco/)

Perhaps you are particularly interested in World Heritage sites. These include monuments, designated ecosystems, and other historical sites that are chosen as important to world heritage. You could develop a research question such as:

What factors affect which sites are chosen by UNESCO as World Heritage sites?

One way to study this would be to compare sites that have been chosen, or compare sites that were chosen with those that were not chosen.

Source for Choosing Cases and Gathering Information

http://whc.unesco.org/en/list

The World Heritage List includes 890 properties forming part of the cultural and natural heritage that are considered to have outstanding universal value.

GENERAL DATA SOURCES FOR CHOOSING CASES AND GATHERING EVIDENCE

The following sources will help you gather information on global economics.

- *Global Transformations Website* (maintained by David Held, Political Science, London School of Economics, and Anthony McGrew, International Relations, Southampton University)—Resources for the study of globalization.
  http://www.polity.co.uk/global/research.asp
- *The Globalization Website*, maintained by Frank Lechner (Emory University).
  http://plato.stanford.edu/entries/globalization/
- *Stanford Encyclopedia of Philosophy, Globalization overview*
  http://plato.stanford.edu/entries/globalization/

Writing Resources

This section contains information that will help you with the research and writing process. It covers how to keep track of your resources, cite appropriately, and follow some style notes specific to international relations research papers.

Chapter 10 discusses how to organize your resources and notes. It contains a quiz that will help you choose the system that is best for you. These organizational systems include the use of note cards, written or electronic journals, and computer software.

Chapter 11 covers when and how to cite your sources properly. The acknowledgment of others' works is not only standard in academia but also a matter of the ethical treatment of intellectual property. This chapter covers the most prominent styles used in international relations: the Turabian and American Psychological Association (APA) styles.

Chapter 12 gives you specific academic style notes, including how to use gender-neutral terminology, capitalize names, refer to treaties and parties, and format foreign words.

Organizing Sources and Notes

Keeping track of your resources and notes is one of the most challenging but important skills to develop as you conduct your research. You can spare yourself countless hours of reorganizing sources or searching for something you know you have read somewhere if you start with an organizational system that works for you. This section walks you through a few ways to organize your notes. In order to determine the most efficient organizational system for you, take the quiz presented here. Once you determine what system you want to use, stick with it and be conscientious about keeping to it.

Research Organization Quiz

For each item, please select the answer that fits you best.

1. I tend to work in a number of different places.
   A. Often.
   B. Sometimes.
   C. Never—I'm always in the same spot.
2. I tend to work with my computer right by my side.
   A. Never.
   B. Sometimes, but not always—for example, sometimes I take reading to do outside.
   C. Often. I am hardly ever without my computer.
   D. Always—when I'm working, I have my computer.
3. I tend to write down ideas about my research and paper.
   A. During my specifically defined research or study time.
   B. Whenever I get the chance.
4. I have a portable device such as an iPod or iPad.
   A. No.
   B. Yes, but I don't always have it with me.
   C. Yes, and it's pretty much always with me.

5. I am comfortable reading journal articles online.
    A. Not really.
    B. I have no preference.
    C. Yes, it's easier.
6. I am comfortable with computer databases.
    A. Not really.
    B. Somewhat.
    C. Yes.
7. I am most comfortable with the following note-taking system:
    A. I am not comfortable with any note-taking system.
    B. Using note cards.
    C. Keeping a research journal.
    D. Using a computer software program (Zotero, Take Note!, EndNote, ProCite, and Reference Manager).

Now add up your score, giving yourself 1 point for every A, 2 points for B, 3 points for C, and 4 points for D. If you scored 7–12 points, you should consider using note cards to organize your research. If you scored 13–18 points, you should consider using a journal or portable device (such as an iPod) with app. If you scored 19–23 points, you should consider using a computer software program.

USING NOTE CARDS

Believe it or not, note cards are still one of the easiest ways to organize your research. A good note card system will allow you to organize notes to easily follow a written outline and will ensure that you can easily put together your reference list or bibliography upon completion of your project. You may even find that a note card reference system can be of assistance to you when writing future papers on a related topic because notes taken for one paper will be easily accessible for another, thereby saving you the time and labor of relocating relevant resources.

Here is how a note card reference system works. Each time you use a book, journal, newspaper, website, or other reference source, fill out a 3×5 note card with the reference's citation information written just as it will be written in your final paper. This may seem time consuming because it requires that you use your style manual during the research process. (We suggest that you use *A Manual for Writers of Research Papers, Theses, and Dissertations* by Kate Turabian [2007] for your references; see Chapter 11 for additional information on citations.) Create a separate but single note card for each resource you use during the course of your research. The actual research notes you take for use in your research paper should be placed on additional note cards.

When using a note card system, you will have many note cards—perhaps dozens—from each individual resource. That is because a good note card system separates out information so that it can easily be sorted for different purposes later in your research project's development. Use separate note cards for each quote; use separate cards to remember different theories; use separate cards for different conclusions or ideas that you find to be relevant.

Multiple note cards will be easy to keep track of if you link each note card to an initial citation card. In most cases, placing the author's last name and first initial in the left-hand corner of the card should be adequate to match your notes to your initial citation card. (See Figure 10.1.) Always include a page number for any notes you take, even if your notes are summary information and not a quote.

It is wise to get in the habit of always using quotation marks if you are directly quoting an author and never using them if you are paraphrasing. Then you will never run the risk of thinking weeks down the road that your notes represented a summary when you actually had recorded direct quotes.

It is possible that you will use resources that have no named author, such as a newspaper article or a website. In these cases, instead of the author's name in the left-hand corner of your research card, place the first few words of the title. Sometimes using the date will work, but this can be problematic if other

> *Goldstein, Joshua S. International*
> *Relations. New York: Longman,*
> *1999.*

> *Goldstein, J.*   *p. 513*
>
> *"Capitalism is a system of private*
> *ownership of capital that relies on*
> *market forces to govern the distri-*
> *bution of goods."*

FIGURE 10.1
Example of an Initial Citation Note Card (*top*) and a Linked Quotation Card (*bottom*).

resources also have the same date. To be on the safe side, we recommend using the title (newspaper headline, website title) and a date whenever there is no clear authorship. The goal is to be able to use a marker that easily links notes with citation cards while avoiding writing lengthy citation information over and over again. If you use several articles or books by the same author, add a letter code to the name or a date so that you can tell which reference is which. For instance, if you used material from four books written by Joshua Goldstein, you might label the first one Goldstein(a), the second one Goldstein(b), and so on. If all of Goldstein's books were published in different years, using the name and publication year would also suffice (e.g., Goldstein 1999 and Goldstein 2003).

The biggest advantage of using a note card system is that when it comes time to write your paper, it is extremely easy to organize your notes. You can go through your cards and sort them into piles that relate to specific aspects of your project. For instance, you can sort your note cards into piles that relate to certain variables, or you can segregate particular quotes and information that you want to use in specific sections of your paper. You can also group related information, such as all the quotes from people who support an issue and all the quotes from people who oppose it. This ends up being much easier than riffling through pages of downloaded material, over and over again, each time picking out different information. Gathering information for your bibliography is extraordinarily easy because you can simply place all of the citation cards together for easy documentation. Some software packages, such as Take Note! by Academix, even allow you to create note cards, bibliographic cites, and outlines for your final paper.

USING A WRITTEN OR ELECTRONIC JOURNAL

You can also keep track of your research by using a journal. Divide a notebook into various sections, and place your notes about different articles, theories, and so on in specific sections. You can create a referencing and page-numbering system by putting all bibliographic citations in one section and recording the information just as you would if you used note cards. The downside to this method comes at the writing stage, when you need to combine material from various sections. This method does not lend itself to the same ease of mixing, matching, and sorting thoughts and resources as can be accomplished with a note card system.

A useful compromise between a journal and a note card system is to type your summaries and notes directly into a personal computer. For an electronic journal, use the same method of recording the bibliographic citations you would use with note cards, and then make a reference to the related citation beside any of the information you gather. By using this method, you can later arrange your notes by electronically cutting and pasting them into groups or in an order that simplifies the writing process.

If you use an iPod, iPad, or other portable device, you may want to explore apps for note taking, note cards, and scheduling. The basic ideas about taking notes apply. You need to collect all relevant information (see the section above about note cards). Also, make sure that you can transfer information on your portable device to your computer. At some point you will need to organize the written product.

The bottom line for your entire research gathering is to develop a consistent system of note taking whereby you always record information the same way each time you sit down to take notes. In sum, always include the source's page numbers near the entry where you record your note, quote, or summary information. Always put quotation marks around anything you copy directly from another source, even if you plan to paraphrase it later. And if you use several sources written by the same author, always use the author's name and the year of the publication to help you keep track of which work you are referencing.

USING SOFTWARE

For students who prefer to take notes on the computer, specialized software may help you manage your resources. This software can be divided into three basic groups: software that facilitates note taking; software that helps keep track of sources and creates bibliographies in a number of different formats; and software that does both. Note-taking software allows you to write notes on your computer and to cut and paste from journal articles and other information found online. This type of software does not necessarily link notes to bibliographic cites. Bibliographic software allows you to keep track of sources but does not necessarily allow you to link your notes to the sources. This software can be used to create bibliographies. Just make sure that you check to see which formats are available. Most contain American Psychological Association (APA) and Modern Language Association (MLA) formats, although it is becoming more common to also find software that includes the formats based on Turabian's book or *The Chicago Manual of Style* (see Chapter 11 for more about styles). Finally, the third type of software, which combines note taking and bibliographic management, contains some nice features, but make sure that you find a program that does not contain too much detail. Some of these programs were created for high-level researchers in certain areas such as science and may not be suited to your needs as a student.

One of the nicest features of all of these programs is that if you have your notes on your computer, you can use the search feature of these programs to find information quickly and efficiently when writing your paper. One drawback that comes with note-taking programs, however, is that students may inadvertently use direct quotations improperly or unethically because it is so easy to cut and paste. Your obligation to the proper acknowledgment of authors is not diminished, however, so you need to take care to cite appropriately. Another drawback to using software programs is that you need to take notes with your computer by your side.

MORE SUGGESTIONS FOR KEEPING TRACK OF RESOURCES

Keeping Track of Print Resources

When taking notes from a book, you can substitute a photocopy of the title page for your citation note card. The title page contains all of the information you will need to write your bibliography or reference list. The only important component missing from the title page is the publication date. Thus, if you use a photocopy of a title page instead of writing a citation note card, be sure to write the year of publication on the photocopy (Figure 10.2).

Edited books require an additional step. An edited volume is generally a collection of chapters written by different authors. Citations for an edited book require the editor's name, the book title, the chapter author's name, and

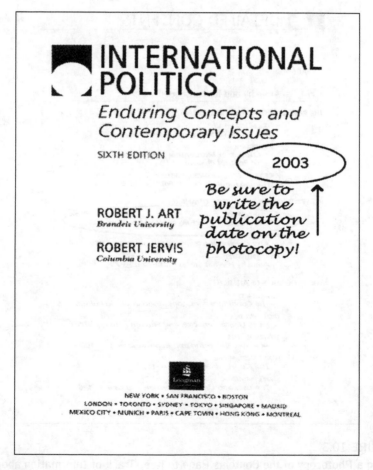

FIGURE 10.2
Using a Photocopy of a Title Page to Keep Track of Citation Information.

the chapter title. Therefore, to have all the information available that you will later need for your bibliography, make a copy of the title page (with the year of publication written on the copy) and a copy of the table of contents. On the copy of the contents page, circle the chapter(s) you used (Figure 10.3). More information about citing this type of resource is included in Chapter 11.

If you have grown accustomed to writing your research papers by organizing photocopies or printouts of articles, books, or downloaded information, moving to a note-taking system as we suggest will seem far too time consuming and awkward at first. But once you are used to such a system, you will find that it makes the writing process much, much easier for the types of complex projects you will soon be exploring in upper-division courses.

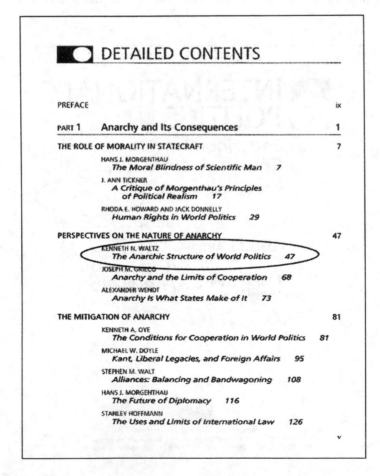

DETAILED CONTENTS

FIGURE 10.3
Using a Photocopy of the Contents Page to Keep Track of Information about a Chapter within an Edited Book.

Keeping Track of Web Resources

Web resources are sometimes quite difficult to keep track of for several reasons. First, Internet websites change constantly. Material you obtain one day may not be there the next. If you take notes from a website, you need to record the page address along with the date that you took your notes (Figure 10.4). Always put the access date on your bibliography card.

You will also need to be careful about the path you take to find Internet resources; otherwise, your bibliography citation may be incorrect. For instance, your school library may offer you a number of different search engines that will take you to various electronically published information, including journal articles, data sources, and credible websites. But many of these resources are not available unless you specifically go through your library home page. If this is the case, you must note the path you took to access the information. The reason is that your scholarship should be available for review by your professor and other scholars who may want to check the accuracy of quotations, your paraphrasing, and your summarization. Remember that it is always better to include too much citation information than too little. So when taking notes, record all information you think you would need later to retrace your research steps and relocate resources. If you can see that the article was also available in hard copy but you read the article online, be sure to note this fact as well.

Organizing your research process takes thought and follow-through but is well worth the effort. You will be ready when you need to cite your sources. Chapter 11 gives you some help on how to do this.

According to Garth Faeth and Suzie Greenhalgh, authors of
A Climate and Environmental Strategy for U.S. Agriculture

"If the Kyoto Protocol of the UNFCC were combined with the right set of domestic agric. policies, net farm cash could actually increase while protecting the climate and improving water quality."

Accessed from http:www.wri.org/press/ces_ag2html
July 5, 2001

FIGURE 10.4
Keeping Track of Print Resources.

Citing Sources

Anumber of different citation styles exist, and many professors and departments prefer a particular citation style for research papers. You should always check with your professors to find out their preference. In this chapter, we briefly review some general rules about what to cite and two of the most commonly used systems in international relations research papers: the Turabian and American Psychological Association (APA) styles.

AVOIDING PLAGIARISM

You must take the issue of citations seriously. Citing the work of others is extremely important. A paper that lacks citations will have little credibility and will raise questions of plagiarism and sloppy research. In general, deciding what needs a citation and what does not is a relatively easy task. Anytime you use another author's work or include statistics and data that are not considered to be common knowledge, you must provide a citation. That rule holds whether you *directly quote, paraphrase, or use another author's work* in your paper. It is unlikely that you will be criticized for too many citations, but you could be accused of ethical violations if you fail to give credit where credit is due.

Most college students behave ethically and would never consider taking another person's work and presenting it as their own. All institutions expect you to abide by academic honor codes governing writing and research.

GENERAL RULES FOR WHAT TO CITE

In general, it is not necessary to provide a citation for data and statistics that are common knowledge or for data and statistics that are not considered subject to change or interpretation. In other words, you do not need to provide a reference when you say that the average body temperature is 98.6 degrees. Nor do you need to provide a reference for such trivial statistics as mileage between cities (or other encyclopedia-type facts). But you *do* need to provide references for data and statistics that are critical to your research, are subject to change, are subject to interpretation, or are dependent on research design (e.g., sample size, population selection, timing). *What gets counted and who does the counting matters!*

Always provide citations for the following:

- Statistical information and data that are not considered common knowledge
- All direct quotes
- References to theories—even those commonly referred to in the international relations literature
- Any conclusions reached by other researchers, whether directly quoted or paraphrased
- References to information found in newspapers and magazines so your readers can verify the information and read the entire article if they wish

Newspaper charts and graphs often use data from a variety of sources. Because you will not know which data came from what source, you need to provide a reference for the information found in the newspaper. If a newspaper study references a specific organization or report where the writer acquired his or her data, you should acknowledge that source in your paper while still citing the newspaper source.

For example, suppose that you read the article noted here:

Jesdanun, Anick. 2003. "TV, radio top sources for breaking news." *News and Record* (Greensboro, NC). August 31.

This Associated Press release begins with the following first paragraph:

In the event of another terror attack, most Americans plan to turn on their televisions and radios before going online or contacting government agencies for information, according to a survey released Saturday.

Rather than simply including this quote in your research on terrorism, it would be better to read more carefully, noting who exactly conducted the survey referred to in the article. Then you could say the following:

A recent report released by the Pew Internet and American Life Project and the *Federal Computer Week* magazine found that "in the event of another terror attack, most Americans plan to turn on their televisions and radios before going online or contacting government agencies for information" (*News and Record* [Greensboro, NC], August 31, 2003) .

Another alternative would be to put additional information on the data in a footnote.

Providing the source of the study in addition to the newspaper citation is important for two reasons. First, the *News and Record* did not conduct the study, so giving just the newspaper as the source would be misleading to readers. Second, the findings were cited as providing new insight into how people will react to a terrorist attack, which means some sources out there may contradict (or at least differ from) these findings. *If in doubt, provide a citation.*

TURABIAN STYLE

If your professor does not insist on a particular style, we recommend that you use the style guide by Kate Turabian (2007), *A Manual for Writers of Research Papers, Theses, and Dissertations* (often simply referred to as "Turabian"), which is an adaptation of *The Chicago Manual of Style*. This is one of the American Political Science Association's preferred guides. Students seem to like it because, in addition to a lot of valuable information about the proper construction of papers, it contains numerous examples of bibliographic citations, footnotes, endnotes, and parenthetical citations (in-text references). Turabian includes examples for the easiest forms of citations as well as really difficult cases (we list a few of these below).

The Basic Citation for a Book

One of the first decisions you will need to make about your written paper is whether you will use parenthetical citations with a reference list *or* footnotes with a bibliography. Sometimes your professor will have a preference, and you should adhere to that. If you get to choose, it is simply a matter of your preference. Some people like parenthetical citations with reference lists because they can see the authors' last names right in the text. Other people prefer footnotes and a bibliography because they believe the text flows better when source information appears in footnotes instead of in the main text. Reference lists serve the same purpose as bibliographies but use a slightly different form. The following general example for a book with one author is meant only to point out the main differences between the two formats. (In our examples in this chapter, First Name and Last Name refer to the name of the author.)

Parenthetical Citation

(Last Name year, page cited)

Reference List

Last Name, First Name. Year. *Title of the book: Subtitle too*. City of Publication: Publisher.

Footnote

[1]First Name Last Name, *Title of the Book: Subtitle Too* (City of Publication: Publisher, year), page cited.

Bibliography

Last Name, First Name. *Title of the Book: Subtitle Too*. City of Publication: Publisher, year.

Using Parenthetical Citations   Parenthetical referencing is a system used within the text to give readers the author's last name, the year of publication, and the page number(s) from the original work. In your paper, you would place the citation after the quoted text, as in this example:

> One researcher writes, "In general, bureaucratic rivalry as an influence on foreign policy challenges the notion of states as unitary actors in the international system" (Goldstein 2003, 168).

If you use parenthetical referencing, you need to include an alphabetical reference list at the end of your paper. The reference list entry for the citation above would look like this:

> Goldstein, Joshua S. 2003. *International relations*. 5th ed. New York: Longman.

Using Footnotes Using footnotes is another form of citation. Word processing programs will automatically number footnotes as you place them in the text. Here's an example of how the footnote marker would look in the text:

> One researcher writes, "In general, bureaucratic rivalry as an influence on foreign policy challenges the notion of states as unitary actors in the international system."[1]

The footnote reference, placed at the bottom of the page, would look like this:

> [1]Joshua S. Goldstein, *International Relations*, 5th ed. (New York: Longman, 2003), 168.

If you use footnotes, then use a bibliography to compile the list of your resources. The bibliography reference for the footnote would look like this:

> Goldstein, Joshua S. *International Relations*. 5th ed. New York: Longman, 2003.

Some scholars prefer footnotes because this method, in addition to providing the reader with complete reference information without making the reader turn to a different page, also allows the author to include further material for the reader without having to add every detail to the text. Here's an example of using a footnote this way:

> One characteristic of the Cold War was American and Soviet support for proxy wars.[2]

The footnote at the bottom of the page could provide further information:

> [2]Proxy wars were wars in the third world in which the United States and the Soviet Union became involved through the supply of weaponry and advisors.

Often, by adding a footnote, you can clarify the use of a term or concept or avoid text that seems to ramble. Footnotes are also useful for indicating that there may be alternative views not covered in your text.

Hard Cases

Component Parts How should you cite from an edited book in which the author of a chapter is different from the editors of the book? Turabian refers to this as a component part by one author in a work by another author. In this case, your bibliography should contain a reference for the entire book as well as a reference for the specific chapter (the component part) you refer to in your paper.

Citing a Component Part

Footnote

¹Robert G. Herman, "Identity, Norms, and National Security: The Soviet Foreign Policy Revolution and the End of the Cold War," in *The Culture of National Security: Norms and Identity in World Politics*, ed. Peter J. Katzenstein (New York: Columbia University Press, 1996), 297.

Bibliography

Herman, Robert G. "Identity, Norms, and National Security: The Soviet Foreign Policy Revolution and the End of the Cold War." In *The Culture of National Security: Norms and Identity in World Politics*, edited by Peter J. Katzenstein, 271–316. New York: Columbia University Press, 1996.

Here are some things to remember about citing a component part:

- Titles of chapters are contained in quotes.
- Titles of books are italicized.
- If you're using parenthetical citations in your paper, use the name of the author who wrote the chapter, not the name of the editor of the book. For instance, continuing with the previous example, the parenthetical citation would be this: (Herman 1996, 297).

Secondary Sources of Quotations You're using a secondary source of a quotation when you repeat a quote you found somewhere other than in the original (primary) source. Whenever you do this, *you must give credit to the original source of the quotation*, not just where you found it. That means looking in your source's footnotes and bibliography to learn where the author found this quote. Citing this is a little tricky. Here's an example.

Secondary Source of a Quotation

Footnote

¹Hans Morgenthau, *Politics Among Nations: The Struggle for Power and Peace*, 6th ed. (New York: Alfred A. Knopf, 1985), 212; quoted in Charles W. Kegley, Jr., and Gregory A. Raymond, *How Nations Make Peace* (New York: St. Martin's, 1999), 164.

Bibliography

Morgenthau, Hans. *Politics Among Nations: The Struggle for Power and Peace*. 6th ed. New York: Alfred A. Knopf, 1985, 212. Quoted in Charles W. Kegley, Jr., and Gregory A. Raymond, *How Nations Make Peace*. New York: St. Martin's, 1999, 164.

APA STYLE

APA style is another citation style used often in the social sciences. The details of this style are contained in the *Publication Manual of the American Psychological Association*, by the American Psychological Association (2001). This style uses parenthetical citations within the text and a reference list at the end of the paper. We present a few basic examples here.

Book with Multiple Authors

Last Name, A.A., Last Name, B.B., & Last Name, C.C. (year). *Title of the book: Subtitle too*. City of Publication: Publisher.

Example

Keck, M., & Sikkink, K. (2006). *Activists beyond borders*. Ithaca, NY: Cornell University Press.

Article in Scholarly Journal

Last Name, A.A., Last Name, B.B., & Last Name, C.C. (year). Title of article. *Title of Periodical, volume number*(issue), pages.

Example

Coyne, C.J. (2006). Reconstructing weak and failed states: Foreign intervention and the nirvana fallacy. *Foreign Policy Analysis*. 2(4), 343–360.

Essay in a Collected Volume

Last Name, A.A., Last Name, B.B., & Last Name, C.C. (year). Title of essay or chapter. In E.E. Editor Name (Ed.), *Title of collection* (pages). City of Publication: Publisher.

Example

Price, R., & Tannenwald, N. (1996). Norms and deterrence: The nuclear and chemical weapons taboos. In P.J. Katzenstein (Ed.),*The culture of national security: Norms and identity in world politics* (pp. 114–152). New York: Columbia University Press.

CITATIONS FOR ONLINE SOURCES

Citing online sources is a bit different from citing other sources because you do not have page numbers, but you do have to include the full URL and the date that you accessed the material online.

The style outlined in *The Columbia Guide to Online Style*, by Walker and Taylor (2006), is often used in social science papers. We recommend the use of this manual to address the complexities associated with online citation. Here are two basic templates. Note that many websites don't list the names of the authors who wrote site material, so if you can't find an author name to start the citation, use the name of the person or organization that owns the site.

Online Source

Last Name, First Name. "Title of the Document or Page." *Title of the Site* [if different]. Date of publication or last revision [if given]. Complete address, including any paths or directories (date of access).

Examples

American Political Science Association. "APSA Task Force on Graduate Education." 23 March 2004. http://www.apsanet.org/imgtest/graduateeducation.pdf (19 June 2007).

U.S. National Archives. "A Brief History." *Presidential Libraries.* http://www.archives.gov/presidential-libraries/about/history.html (19 June 2007).

Article from Online Database or Electronic Publication

Last Name, First Name. "Title of the Article." *Title of Publication* [if given]. Any identifying information, such as volume number, date, and pages of print version. File number [if available]. *Name of database* [if different from the publication]. *Name of the online service or Internet address* (date of access).

Example

Feldstein, Martin. "A Self-Help Guide to Emerging Markets." *Foreign Affairs* 78:2 (March/April 1999). *Columbia International Affairs Online,* Columbia University Press. https://wwwc.cc.columbia.edu/sec/dlc/ciao/olj/fa/fa_99fem01.html (29 March 1999).

In the online database example, we accessed a journal article by Martin Feldstein on the Columbia International Affairs Online site. The site contained a link to the preferred citation style shown above.

The American Political Science Association (2006) offers a book titled *The Style Manual for Political Science*, which you can purchase through the association's website (http://www.apsanet.org). The American Psychological Association has an online guide to citing electronic resources: http://www.apastyle.org/elecref.html.

You may also want to consult Wienbroer (2001), *Rules of Thumb for Online Research.*

REMEMBER THE BASICS

You can easily construct accurate citations by following Turabian or any other assigned or acceptable style guide. Here are a few tips to remember.

- Reference lists and bibliographies should be in alphabetical order.
- Footnotes use commas. Bibliographies and reference lists use periods.
- Book titles are italicized. Titles within a book, magazine, or journal are not italicized, but in some styles they are put within quotation marks.

- Reference lists put the year after the author's name. Bibliographies put the year at the end of the citation.
- Footnotes indent the first line. Bibliographies and reference lists use hanging indents (all lines but the first are indented).
- It is advisable to always use the year of publication along with your parenthetical citation even if you use only one publication from the author.
- In a bibliography or a reference list, the entry begins with the author's last name, followed by a comma and the first name. In a footnote, use the first name and then the last name. A parenthetical citation starts with the author's last name but doesn't use the first name.
- Entries for more than one article or book by the same author should be ordered by year, beginning with the most recent. If you cite two sources published in the same year by the same author, provide a letter beside the year to clarify to which citation you are referring (e.g., 2000, 2000a, 2000b).

Following Style Guidelines

This section contains important style notes on writing that will help you as you construct your research paper. Here we focus on academic writing within the discipline of international relations.

ACADEMIC WRITING

Your writing should have an academic tone and style. What does that mean? Your paper is a scholarly discussion of your topic. To be taken seriously, you must be serious about your writing. Here are a few things to remember.

1. Write clear and complete sentences.
2. Avoid slang and jargon.
3. Avoid the use of personal pronouns.
4. Avoid phrases such as "I feel" or "I believe."
5. Think about the structure of your paragraphs. Does each paragraph contain a topic sentence? Does the paragraph stick to that topic?
6. Proofread your paper (don't simply spell-check it with a computer) to make sure the spelling and grammar are correct.

GENDER-NEUTRAL TERMINOLOGY

The American Political Science Association asks that authors adopt gender-neutral language. One strategy is to use words that do not suggest gender.

Example
Gender Distinctive
Citizens elect congressmen to serve in Washington.

Gender Neutral
Citizens elect congressional representatives to serve in Washington.

Gender Distinctive
The number of man-hours needed for implementation will soon exceed the personnel and financial capacities of the troubled agency.

Gender Neutral
The number of staff-hours needed for implementation will soon exceed the personnel and financial capacities of the troubled agency.

Another strategy is to eliminate pronouns if possible.

Example
Gender Distinctive
If a citizen votes, he does participate in the process.

Gender Neutral
A citizen who votes does participate in the process.

A third strategy is to replace "he" with "he or she," or "his" with "his or her."

Example
Gender Distinctive
It is always wise to consult with your professor for his preference.

Gender Neutral
It is always wise to consult with your professor for his or her preference.

GENERAL RULES ON CAPITALIZATION FOR LEADERS' TITLES

Leadership titles are not treated as proper nouns and are not capitalized unless referring to specific people. Thus, if you mention a specific political leader (e.g., a particular president, chief executive, prime minister, legislator, judge, etc.), capitalize the title. If you are writing about a type of leader in general, do not capitalize. Note, however, that you should always use a capital C in the phrase "member of Congress" because "Congress" itself is a proper name.

Example
That is generally subject to the discretion of the president.

That is generally subject to President Bush's discretion.

Although the president has the power to make treaties, Congress must ratify the treaty.

Even though he knew Congress would disapprove, the President signed the treaty.

A senator is not required to respond.

No one knows why Senator Smith did not respond.

In general, prime ministers do not attend the funerals of low-level dignitaries.

Soon after his speech, the Prime Minister returned to his seat.

The responsibilities of the chief executive include. . . .

There is no response from the Chief Executive at this time.

The first time that you mention a specific person in your paper, use his or her full name and title. Subsequently, you may use only the last name. For example, at the first instance, write, "Prime Minster Gordon Brown." After that, you can refer to him as "Brown."

PARTIES, THE CONSTITUTION, AND TREATIES

When referring to a political party, you should capitalize the name (e.g., Republican, Democratic, Reform, Socialist, Green), but use lowercase letters when these terms refer to a philosophy or form of government.

Examples
The republican principles of community participation were encouraged.
An initiative backed by the Republican Party swept through the committee.

He wanted a more democratic process.

The Democrats did not favor the changes.

When referring to the U.S. Constitution, always capitalize it as shown here. Capitalize when you are referring to a specific treaty but not when discussing treaties in general.

Examples
The number of treaties signed has increased.

The United States withdrew from the Antiballistic Missile Treaty effective in mid-2002.

PROPER NOUNS AND ADJECTIVES

Capitalize proper nouns and adjectives made from these nouns.

Examples
Russia

Russian dignitaries

Also capitalize historical events or calendar dates as well as names of monuments or buildings.

Examples
World War I

September 11, 2001

the Kremlin

Whitehall

the Washington Monument

the Statue of Liberty

Capitalize the names of international organizations.

Examples
the World Bank
the World Health Organization (WHO)
the United Nations (UN)

Remember to use the full name of an organization before you use the acronym, and do not use acronyms at the beginning of a sentence.

TITLES OF NEWSPAPERS

Italicize newspaper titles in your research paper. When proper syntax calls for the use of the word "the" to precede the title, "the" is generally not capitalized in the text.

Examples
A recent article in the *New York Times* reported that. . . .
According to the *News and Observer*, . . .

For additional information on capitalization, see the guidelines available at the Online Writing Lab of Purdue University (http://owl.english.purdue.edu/index.htm).

FOREIGN WORDS

Italicize any foreign words that you use in your paper.

Examples
glasnost
perestroika
modus operandi

RECOMMENDED WRITING AND STYLE MANUALS

American Political Science Association. 2006. *The style manual for political science*. Washington, DC: American Political Science Association.
Strunk, William, Jr., and E. B. White. 1999. *The elements of style: A style guide for writers*. 4th ed. Upper Saddle River, NJ: Pearson Education.
Turabian, Kate L. 2007. *A manual for writers of research papers, theses, and dissertations*. 7th ed. Chicago: University of Chicago Press.

REFERENCES

Abdelal, Rawi, Mark Blyth, and Craig Parsons. 2010. *Constructing the international economy.* Ithaca, NY: Cornell University Press.

Aidt, Toke S. 2009. Corruption, institutions, and economic development. *Oxford Review of Economic Policy,* 25(2): 271–291.

Ali, Taisier M., and Robert O. Matthews, eds. 1999. *Civil wars in Africa: Roots and resolution.* Montreal: McGill-Queen's University Press.

Allison, Graham T., and Philip Zelikow. 1999. *Essence of decision: Explaining the Cuban missile crisis.* 2nd ed. New York: Longman.

American Political Science Association. 2006. *The style manual for political science.* Washington, DC: American Political Science Association.

American Psychological Association. 2001. *Publication manual of the American Psychological Association.* 5th ed. Washington, DC: American Psychological Association.

Arnull, Anthony. 2006. *The European Union and its Court of Justice,* 2nd ed. Oxford: Oxford University Press.

Ashworth, G.J., and J.E. Tunbridge, 1999. Old cities, new pasts: Heritage planning in selected cities of Central Europe, *GeoJournal,* 49: 105–116.

Axelrod, Regina S., David L. Downie, and Norman J. Vig., eds. 2005. 2nd ed. *The global environment: Institutions, law, and policy.* Washington, DC: Congressional Quarterly Press.

Barro, Robert J. 1997. *Determinants of economic growth: A cross-country empirical study.* Cambridge, MA: MIT Press.

Barry, John, and Gene Frankland. 2002. *International encyclopedia of environmental politics.* London: Routledge.

Bar-Siman-Tov, Yaacov. 2004. *From conflict resolution to reconciliation.* New York: Oxford University Press.

Bendor, Jonathan, and Thomas H. Hammond. 1992. Rethinking Allison's models. *American Political Science Review* 86: 301–22.

Beneria, Lourdes. 2003. *Gender, development, and globalization: Economics as if all people mattered.* New York: Routledge.

Bennett, W. Lance. 2003. New media power: The Internet and global activism. In Nick Couldry and James Curran (eds.) *Contesting media power,* pp. 17–37. Lanham, MD: Rowman & Littlefield.

———. 2005. Social movements beyond borders: Understanding two eras of transnational activism. In Donatella Della Porta and Sidney Tarrow (eds.) *Transnational protest and global activism,* pp. 203–226. Lanham, MD: Rowman & Littlefield.

Bercovitch, Jacob, and Richard Jackson. 1997. *International conflict: A chronological encyclopedia of conflicts and their management 1945–1995.* Washington, DC: Congressional Quarterly.

Betsill, Michele M., Kathryn Hochstetler, and Dimitris Stevis, eds. 2006. *International environmental politics.* New York: Palgrave Macmillan.

Bhagwati, Jagdish. 2004. *In defense of globalization*. New York: Oxford University Press.

Biersteker, T. J., and C. Weber, eds. 1996. *State sovereignty as social construct*. Cambridge, UK: Cambridge University Press.

Blustein, Paul. 2009. *Misadventures of the most favored nations: Clashing egos, inflated ambitions, and the great shambles of the world trade system*. New York: PublicAffairs.

Brecher, Michael, and Jonathan Wilkenfeld. 1997. *A study of crisis*. Ann Arbor: University of Michigan Press.

Brown, Michael E., ed. 1996. *The international dimensions of internal conflict*. Cambridge, MA: MIT Press.

Brown, Michael E., Owen R. Cote, Jr., Sean M. Lynn-Jones, and Steven E. Miller, eds. 1997. *Nationalism and ethnic conflict*. Cambridge, MA: MIT Press.

Brysk, Alison. 2002. *Globalization and human rights*. Berkeley: University of California Press.

Byers, Michael. 2005. *War law: Understanding international law and armed conflict*. Berkeley, CA: Grove Press.

Byman, Daniel L., and Kenneth M. Pollack. 2001. Let us now praise great men: Bringing the statesman back in. *International Security* 25(4): 107–46.

Caporaso, James A., and David P. Levine. 1993. *Theories of political economy*. New York: Cambridge University Press.

Carbone, Maurizio. 2007. *The European Union and international development: the politics of foreign aid*. New York: Routledge.

Castles, Stephen, Mark J. Miller, and Giuseppe Ammendola. 2003. *The age of migration: International population movements in the modern world*. New York: The Guilford Press.

Cha, Victor D. 2000. Globalization and the study of international security. *Journal of Peace Research* 37(3): 391–403.

Chape, Stuart, Mark Spalding, and Martin Jenkins. 2008. *The world's protected areas: Status, values and prospects in the 21st century*. Univ de Castilla La Mancha.

Chorev, Nitsan. 2007. *Remaking U.S. trade policy: From protectionism to globalization*. Ithaca, NY: Cornell University Press.

Cohn, Theodore. 2003. *Global political economy: Theory and practice*. New York: Longman.

Collier, Paul and Nicholas Sambanis. 2005. *Understanding civil war: Evidence and analysis*. Washington, D.C.: World Bank Publications.

Combs, Cynthia C. 1997. *Terrorism in the twenty-first century*. Upper Saddle River, NJ: Prentice Hall.

Conway, Maura. 2007 *Terrorism, the Internet, and international relations: The governance conundrum*. In Dunn Cavelty, Myriam and Mauer, Victor and Krishna-Hensel, Sai Felicia (eds.) Power and security in the information age: Investigating the role of the state in cyberspace, pp. 95–127. Burlington, VT: Ashgate Publishing Group.

Cooper, Andrew F., and John J. Kirton. 2009. *Innovation in global health governance*. Burlington, VT: Ashgate Publishing Group.

Crabb, Cecil V., Jr., Glenn J. Antizzo, and Leila E. Sarieddine. 2000. *Congress and the foreign policy process: Modes of legislative behavior*. Baton Rouge: Louisiana State University Press.

Cypher, James M., and James L. Dietz. 2004. *The process of economic development*. 2nd ed. New York: Routledge.

Dauvergne, Catherine. 2008. *Making people illegal: What globalization means for migration and law.* Cambrige: Cambridge University Press.

Deibert, Ronald J., John G. Palfrey, Rafal Rohozinski, and Jonathan Zittrain, eds. 2010 *Access controlled: The shaping of power, rights and rule in cyberspace.* Cambridge, MA: MIT Press.

de Jong, Wilma, Martin Shaw, and Neil Stammers, eds. 2005. *Global activism, global media.* Ann Arbor: Pluto Press.

Deutsch, Morton, Peter T. Coleman, and Eric Colton Marcus. 2006. *The handbook of conflict resolution: Theory and practice,* 2nd ed. Hoboken, NJ: John Wiley and Sons.

Diehl, Paul F., Daniel Druckman, and James Wall. 1998. International peacekeeping and conflict resolution: A taxonomic analysis with implications. *Journal of Conflict Resolution* 42: 33–55.

Dobson, Hugo. 2003. *Japan and UN peacekeeping: New pressures and new responses.* London: Routledge.

Donnelly, Jack. 2006. *International human rights.* Boulder, CO: Westview Press.

Doremus, Paul N., William W. Keller, Louis W. Pauly, and Simon Reich. 1998. *The myth of the global corporation.* Princeton, NJ: Princeton University Press.

Duncan, W. Raymond, Barbara Jancar-Webster, and Bob Switky. 2001. *World politics in the twenty-first century.* New York: Longman.

Durch, William J., ed. 1993. *The evolution of UN peacekeeping: Case studies and comparative analysis.* New York: St. Martin's Press.

Egger, Peter, and Hans Winner. 2005. Evidence on corruption as an incentive for foreign direct investment. *European Journal of Political Economy,* 21, 932–52.

Entman, Robert M. 2004. *Projections of power: Framing news, public opinion, and U.S. foreign policy.* Chicago: University of Chicago Press.

Escobar, Arturo. 1995. *Encountering development: The making and unmaking of the third world.* Princeton, NJ: Princeton University Press.

Esman, Milton J. 1995. *Ethnic politics.* Ithaca, NY: Cornell University Press.

Falk, Richard, Irene Gendzier, and Robert Jay Lifton. 2006. *Crimes of war: Iraq.* New York: Nation Books.

Finnemore, Martha. 1996. *National interests in international society.* Ithaca, NY: Cornell University Press.

———. 2003. *The purpose of intervention.* Ithaca, NY: Cornell University Press.

Finnemore, Martha and Kathryn Sikkink. (1998). International norm dynamics and political change. *International Organization* 52(4): 887–917.

Fisman, Raymond, and Edwar Miguel. 2010. *Economic gangsters: Corruption, violence, and the poverty of nations.* Princeton: Princeton University Press.

Forsythe, David. 2000. *The internationalization of human rights.* Washington, DC: Lexington Books.

Gelleny, Ronald D., and Matthew McCoy. 2001. Globalization and government policy independence: The issue of taxation. *Political Research Quarterly* 54(3): 509–29.

George, Alexander L., and Juliette L. George. 1964. *Woodrow Wilson and Colonel House: A personality study.* New York: Dover Publications.

Gillies, David. 1996. *Between principle and practice: Human rights in North-South relations.* Montreal: McGill-Queen's University Press.

Gilpin, Robert. 1975. *U.S. power and the multinational corporation.* New York: Basic Books.

———. 1987. *The political economy of international relations.* Princeton, NJ: Princeton University Press.

———. 2003. *Global political economy: Understanding the international economic order.* New Delhi: Orient Longman.

Goff, Patricia. 2000. Invisible borders: Economic liberalization and national identity. *International Studies Quarterly* 44(4) (December): 533–63.

Goldstein, Joshua S. 2001. *International relations*. 4th ed. New York: Longman.

———. 2003. *International relations*. 5th ed. New York: Longman.

Graham, Thomas. 1994. Public opinion and U.S. foreign policy decision making. In David A. Deese (ed.). *The new politics of American foreign policy*, 190–215. New York: St. Martin's Press.

Grieco, Joseph, and G. John Ikenberry. 2003. *State power and world markets*. New York: W. W. Norton and Co.

Griffiths, Stephen Iwan. 1993. *Nationalism and ethnic conflict*. New York: Oxford University Press.

Gunn, William A., P. B. Mansourian, Anthony Piel, A. Michael Davies, and Bruce Sayers. 2010. *Understanding the global dimensions of health*. New York: Springer.

Gurr, Ted Robert. 2000. *People versus states: Minorities at risk in the new century*. Washington, DC: United States Institute of Peace Press.

Gurr, Ted Robert, and Barbara Harff. 1994. *Ethnic conflict in world politics*. Boulder, CO: Westview.

Hall, C.M. 2001. World heritage and tourism, *Tourism Recreation Research*, 26(1): 1–3.

Hanhimaki, Jussi M. 2008. *The United Nations: A very short introduction*. Oxford: Oxford University Press.

Hanson, Elizabeth C. 2008. *The information revolution and world politics*. Lanham, MD: Rowman & Littlefield.

Hasenclever, Andreas, Peter Mayer, and Volker Rittberger. 1997. *Theories of international regimes*. New York: Cambridge University Press.

Hawkins, Darren G. 2006. *Delegation and agency in international organizations*. Cambridge: Cambridge University Press.

Held, David. 2002. *Globalization/anti-globalization*. Cambridge: Polity Press.

Hermann, Margaret G. 1980. Explaining foreign policy behavior using the personal characteristics of political leaders. *International Studies Quarterly* 24: 7–46.

Herrick, Christopher, and Patricia B. McRae. 2003. *Issues in American foreign policy*. New York: Longman.

Hoekman, Bernard, and Michel Kostecki. 2010. *The political economy of the world trading system: From GATT to WTO*. 3rd ed. New York: Oxford University Press.

Hoffman, Bruce. 2006. *Inside terrorism*, 2nd ed. New York: Columbia University Press.

Holsti, Ole R. 1996 and 2009 rev. ed. *Public opinion and American foreign policy*. Ann Arbor: University of Michigan Press.

Horowitz, Donald L. 1985. *Ethnic groups in conflict*. Berkeley: University of California Press.

Howard, Michael. 1997. *The laws of war: Constraints on warfare in the western world*. New Haven, CT: Yale University Press.

Hudson, V. M., S. M. Sims, and J. C. Thomas. 1993. The domestic political context of foreign policy-making: Explicating a theoretical construct. In D. Skidmore and V. M. Hudson (eds.) *The limits of state autonomy*, 49–101. Boulder, CO: Westview.

Huth, Paul K. 1998. Major power intervention in international crises, 1918–1988. *The Journal of Conflict Resolution* 42(6): 744–70.

Ikenberry, G. John, ed. 2004. *American foreign policy: Theoretical essays*. New York: Longman.

Ishay, Micheline R. 2008. *The history of human rights: From ancient times to the globalization era*. Berkeley: University of California Press.

Jameson, Kenneth P., and Charles K. Wilber, eds. 1996. *The political* economy of development and under-development. 6th ed. New York: McGraw-Hill.

Jensen, Nathan Michael. 2006. *Nation-states and the multinational corporation: a political economy of foreign direct investment.* Princeton, NJ: Princeton University Press.

Jentleson, Bruce W. 2004. *American foreign policy: The dynamics of choice in the twenty-first century.* New York: W. W. Norton.

Jervis, Robert. 1976. *Perception and misperception in international politics.* Princeton, NJ: Princeton University Press.

Jing, Chao, William H. Kaempfer, and Anton D. Lowenberg. 2003. Instrument choice and the effectiveness of international sanctions: A simultaneous equations approach. *Journal of Peace Research* 40, no. 5: 519–35.

Jones, Kent. 2009. *Who's afraid of the WTO? Doha blues: Institutional crisis and reform in the WTO.* Oxford, UK: Oxford University Press.

Kaldor, Mary. 2007. *New and old wars.* 2nd ed. Cambridge: Polity Press.

Kalyvas, Stathis N. 2001. "New" and "old" civil wars: A valid distinction? *World Politics* 54: 99–118.

Karns, Margaret P., and Karen A. Mingst. 2009. *International organizations: The politics and processes of global governance.* Boulder, CO: Lynne Rienner Publishers.

Keck, Margaret, and Kathryn Sikkink. 1998. *Activists beyond borders: advocacy networks in international politics.* Ithaca, NY: Cornell University Press.

Keegan, John. 1993. *A history of warfare.* New York: Random House.

Keohane, Robert O. 1998. International institutions: Can interdependence work? *Foreign Policy* 110: 82–96.

Keohane, Robert O., Marc A. Levy, and Peter M. Haas. 1993. *Institutions for the earth: Sources of effective international environmental protection.* Cambridge, MA: MIT Press.

Khong, Yuen Foong. 1992. *Analogies at war: Korea, Munich, Dien Bien Phu, and the Vietnam decisions of 1965.* Princeton, NJ: Princeton University Press.

Koehn, Peter H. 2006. Globalization, migration health, and educational preparation for transnational medical encounters. *Globalization and Health* 2(2).

Kohli, Atul. 2004. *State-directed development: Political power and industrialization in the global periphery.* Cambridge: Cambridge University Press.

Koser, Khalid. 2007. *International migration: A very short history.* Oxford: Oxford University Press.

Krasner, Stephen D., ed. 1983. *International regimes.* Ithaca, NY: Cornell University Press.

Kratochwil, Friedrich W. 1989. *Rules, norms, and decisions: On the conditions of practical and legal reasoning in international relations and domestic affairs.* New York: Cambridge University Press.

Kurtz, Lester R., ed. 1999. *Encyclopedia of violence, peace, and conflict.* 3 vols. San Diego, CA: Academic Press.

Leff, Nathaniel. 1964. Economic development through bureaucratic corruption. *American Behavioral Scientist,* 8(3); 8–14.

Levy, Jack. 1997. Prospect theory, rational choice, and international relations. *International Studies Quarterly 41:* 87–112.

Licklider, Roy, ed. 1993. *Stopping the killing: How civil wars end.* New York: New York University Press.

Lobell, Steven. 2004. *Ethnic conflict and international politics: Explaining diffusion and escalation.* New York: Palgrave Macmillan.

Lowe, Vaughan, and Malgosia Fitsmaurice. 2007. *Fifty Years of the International Court of Justice: Essays in Honour of Sir Robert Jennings.* Cambridge: Cambridge University Press.

Luttwak, Edward, and Stuart L. Koehl. 1991. *The dictionary of modern war.* New York: HarperCollins.

Lynch, Timothy J., and Robert S. Singh. 2008. *After Bush: The case for continuity in American foreign policy.* Cambridge: Cambridge University Press.

MacLean, Sandra J., Pieter Fourie, and Sherri Brown, eds. 2009. *Health for some: The political economy of global health governance.* New York: Palgrave.

MacQueen, Norrie. 2002. *United Nations peacekeeping in Africa since 1960.* London: Longman.

Mahler, Sarah J., and Patricia R. Pessar. 2006. Gender matters: Ethnographers bring gender from the periphery toward the core of migration studies. *International Migration Review* 40(1): 27–63.

Mansfield, Edward, and Jack Snyder. 2005. *Electing to fight: Why emerging democracies go to war.* Cambridge, MA: MIT Press.

Massiah, Joycelin, ed. 1992. *Women in developing economies: Making visible the invisible.* New York: Berg.

Mayall, James, ed. 1996. *The new interventionism, 1991–1994: United Nations experience in Cambodia, former Yugoslavia, and Somalia.* New York: Cambridge University Press.

McDermott, Rose. 1998. *Risk-taking in international politics: Prospect theory in American foreign policy.* Ann Arbor: University of Michigan Press.

———. 2004. Prospect theory in political science: Gains and losses from the first decade. *Political Psychology* 25(2): 289–312.

McElroy, Robert. 1993. *Morality and American foreign policy.* Princeton, NJ: Princeton University Press.

McFee, Erin. 2007. *What factors affect U.S. intervention in humanitarian crises?* Paper for Senior Seminar: Interstate Conflict. Elon University.

Mearsheimer, John J. 2001. *The tragedy of great power politics.* New York: W. W. Norton and Company.

Meernik, James. 2003. Victor's justice or the law? Judging and punishing at the International Criminal Tribunal for the former Yugoslavia. *Journal of Conflict Resolution* 47(2): 140–62.

Mehrota, Santosh, and Richard Jolly, eds. 1997. *Development with a human face: Experiences in social achievement and economic growth.* New York: Oxford University Press.

Momsen, Janet Henshall. 2004. *Gender and development.* London: Routledge.

Mott, William. 2004. *Globalization: People, perspectives, and progress.* Westport, CT: Praeger.

Mueller, John. 1994. *Policy and opinion in the Gulf War.* Chicago: University of Chicago Press.

Mueller, Milton. 2010. Networks and States: *The global politics of internet governance.* Cambridge, MA: MIT Press.

Nacos, Bridgette Lebens. 2007. *Mass-mediated terrorism: The central role of the media in terrorism and counterterrorism.* New York: Routledge.

Neack, Laura, Jeanne A. K. Hey, and Patrick J. Haney. 1995. *Foreign policy analysis: Continuity and change in its second generation.* Englewood Cliffs, NJ: Prentice Hall.

Neustadt, Richard, and Ernest R. May. 1986. *Thinking in time: The uses of history for decision makers.* New York: Macmillan USA.

Nussbaum, Martha C. 2000. *Women and human development: The capabilities approach.* Cambridge: Cambridge University Press.

Nye, Joseph S. 2004. *Power in the global information age: From realism to globalization.* London: Routledge.

———. 2007. *Understanding international conflicts: An introduction to theory and history.* 6th ed. Longman Classics Series. New York: Longman.

———. 2010. *Soft power and U.S. foreign policy: Theoretical, historical and contemporary perspectives.* New York: Routledge.

O'Connell, Robert L. 1989. *Of arms and men: A history of war, weapons and aggression.* New York: Oxford University Press.

Oliverio, Annamarie. 1998. *The state of terror.* Albany, NY: SUNY Press.

Osmanczyk, Edmund. 2003. *Encyclopedia of the United Nations and international agreements.* New York: Routledge.

Parpart, Jane L. 2000. Rethinking participation, empowerment, and development from a gender perspective. In Jim Freedman (ed.) *Transforming development: Foreign aid for a changing world*, pp. 250–267. Toronto: University of Toronto Press.

Pearson, Frederic. 2001. Dimensions of conflict resolution in ethnopolitical disputes. *Journal of Peace Research* 38(3): 275–87.

Perry, Michael. 1998. *The idea of human rights: Four inquiries.* New York: Oxford University Press.

Pillar, Paul R. 2003. *Terrorism and U.S. foreign policy.* Washington, DC: Brookings Institution Press.

Powlick, Philip J., and Andrew Z. Katz. 1998. Defining the American public opinion/foreign policy nexus. *International Studies Quarterly* 42: 29–63.

Poynter, Thomas A. 1985. *Multinational enterprises and government intervention.* New York: St. Martin's Press.

Pushkina, Darya. 2006. A recipe for success? Ingredients of a successful peacekeeping mission. *International Peacekeeping* 13(2): 133–149.

Qiang, Christine Zhen–Wei. 2007. China's information revolution: managing the economic and social transformation. Washington DC: World Bank Publications.

Rapoport, David C., ed. 1988. *Inside terrorist organizations.* New York: Columbia University Press.

Ratner, Steven R. 1996. *The new UN peacekeeping: Building peace in lands of conflict after the Cold War.* New York: St. Martin's Press.

Reich, Walter, ed. 1990. *Origins of terrorism: Psychologies, ideologies, theologies, states of mind.* New York: Cambridge University Press.

Risse, Thomas, Stephen C. Ropp, and Kathryn Sikkink, eds. 1999. *The power of human rights: International norms and domestic change.* New York: Cambridge University Press.

Robertson, David. 2000. Civil society and the WTO. *World Economy* 23(9) (September): 1119–34.

Rodrick, Dani. 2008. *One economics, many recipes: Globalization, institutions, and economic growth.* Princeton: Princeton University Press.

Rose-Ackerman, Susan. 1999. *Corruption and government, causes, consequences and reform.* Cambridge: Cambridge University Press.

Rosecrance, Richard. 1987. *The rise of the trading state: Commerce and conquest in the modern world.* New York: Basic Books.

Rousseau, David. 2005. *Democracy and war: Institutions, norms, and the evolution of international conflict.* Stanford, CA: Stanford University Press.

Russett, Bruce. 1994. *Grasping the democratic peace.* Princeton, NJ: Princeton University Press.

Ryan, Jason, and Sari Silvanto. 2009. The World Heritage List: The making and management of a brand. *Place Branding and Public Diplomacy* 5(4): 290–300.

Saari, David J. 1999. *Global corporations and sovereign nations: Collision or cooperation?* Westport,

CT: Quorum Books/Greenwood Publishing Group.

Sally, Razeen. 1995. *States and firms: Multinational enterprises in institutional competition.* New York: Routledge.

Sandole, Dennis J. D., and Hugo van der Merwe. 1993. *Conflict resolution theory and practice: Integration and application.* New York: Manchester University Press.

Schiff, Benjamin. 2008. *Building the international criminal court.* Cambridge: Cambridge University Press.

Schott, Jeffrey J., ed. 2000. *The WTO after Seattle.* Washington, DC: Institute for International Economics.

Scott, Catherine V. 1996. *Gender and development: Rethinking modernization and dependency theory.* Boulder, CO: Lynne Rienner.

Sen, Amartya. 1999. *Development as freedom.* New York: Alfred A. Knopf.

Shanty, Frank, and Raymond Picquet. 2003. *Encyclopedia of world terrorism.* Armonk, NY: Sharpe Reference.

Shapiro, Robert Y., and Benjamin I. Page. 1994. Foreign policy and public opinion. In David A. Deese (ed.) *The new politics of American foreign policy,* 216–35. New York: St. Martin's Press.

Sikkink, Kathryn. 1993. Human rights, principled issue-networks, and sovereignty in Latin America. *International Organization* 47: 411–41.

Simmons, Beth, and Allison Danner. 2010. Credible commitments and the International Criminal Court. *International Organization* 64: 225–256.

Simons, Geoffrey. 1998. *Vietnam Syndrome: Impact on U.S. foreign policy.* New York: St. Martin's Press.

Skidmore, David, and Valerie M. Hudson. 1993. *The limits of state autonomy: Societal groups and foreign policy formation.* Boulder, CO: Westview Press.

Skonieczny, Amy. 2001. Constructing NAFTA: Myth, representation, and the discursive construction of U.S. foreign policy. *International Studies Quarterly* 45(3): 433–454.

Smith, B.C. 2007. *Good governance and economic development.* London: Palgrave.

Spero, Joan, and Jeffrey Hart. 2010. *The politics of international economic relations.* 7th ed. Boston: Wadsworth Cengage Learning.

Stiglitz, Joseph E. 2006. *Making globalization work.* New York: W. W. Norton & Co.

Stoessinger, John G. 2004. *Why nations go to war.* 9th ed. Boston: Bedford/St. Martin's Press.

Strunk, William, Jr., and E. B. White. 1999. *The elements of style: A style guide for writers.* 4th ed. Upper Saddle River, NJ: Pearson Education.

Sutterlin, James. 2003. *The United Nations and the maintenance of international security: A challenge to be met.* Westport, CT: Praeger.

Tarrow, Sidney. 2005. *The new transnational activism.* New York: Cambridge University Press.

Taylor, Andrew J., and John T. Rourke. 1995. Historical analogies in the congressional foreign policy process. *Journal of Politics* 57: 460–68.

Thackrah, John. 2004. *Dictionary of terrorism.* London: Routledge.

Tillema, Herbert K. 1994. Cold War alliance and overt military intervention, 1945–1991. *International Interactions* 20: 249–78.

Towns, Ann E. 2010. *Women and states: Norms and hierarchies in international society.* Cambridge: Cambridge University Press.

Treisman, Daniel. 2007. What have we learned about the causes of corruption from ten years of cross-national empirical research? *Annual Review of Political Science 10:* 211–244.

Turabian, Kate L. 2007. *A manual for writers of research papers, theses, and dissertations.* 7th ed. Chicago: University of Chicago Press.

Van Creveld, Martin. 1989. *Technology and war: From 2000 BC to the present.* New York: Free Press.

Vertzberger, Yaacov Y. I. 1990. *The world in their minds: Information processing, cognition, and perception in foreign policy decision-making.* Stanford, CA: Stanford University Press.

Victor, David G., Kal Raustiala, and Eugene B. Skolnikoff. 1998. *The implementation and effectiveness of international environmental commitments: Theory and practice.* Cambridge, MA: MIT Press.

Voeten, Erik. 2001. Outside options and the logic of Security Council action. *The American Political Science Review 95*: 845–58.

Walker, Janice R., and Todd Taylor. 2006. *The Columbia guide to online style.* New York: Columbia University Press.

Walker, Stephen G., Mark Schafer, and Michael D. Young. 1998. Systematic procedures for operational code analysis: Measuring and modeling Jimmy Carter's operational code. *International Studies Quarterly 42*: 175–89.

Wallensteen, Peter. 2002. *Understanding conflict resolution: War, peace and the global system.* London: Sage.

Waltz, Kenneth N. 1979. *Theory of international politics.* New York: Longman.

Weiss, Linda, ed. 2003. *States in the global economy: Bringing domestic institutions back in.* Cambridge: Cambridge University Press.

Weiss, Thomas G., David P. Forsythe, and Roger A. Coate. 2007. *The United Nations and changing world politics, 5th ed.* Boulder, CO: Westview.

Welch, David A. 1992. The organizational process and bureaucratic politics paradigms: Retrospect and prospect. *International Security 17*: 112–46.

Wendt, Alexander. 1992. Anarchy is what states make of it: The social construction of power politics. *International Organization 46*(2): 391–425.

Western, Jon W. 2005. *Selling intervention and war: The presidency, the media, and the American public.* Baltimore: Johns Hopkins University Press.

Whittacker, David J. 2007. *Terrorism: Understanding the global threat, 2nd ed.* New York: Longman/Pearson.

Wienbroer, Diana Roberts. 2001. *Rules of thumb for online research.* Boston: McGraw-Hill.

Wilson, Ernest J. 2006. *The information revolution and developing countries.* Cambridge, MA: MIT Press.

Wittkopf, Eugene, and James McCormick. 2004. *The domestic sources of American foreign policy: Insights and evidence.* Lanham, MD: Rowman and Littlefield.

Wolff, Stefan. 2006. *Ethnic conflict: A global perspective.* Oxford: Oxford University Press.

Yoon, Mi Yung. 1997. Explaining U.S. intervention in third-world internal wars, 1945–1989. *The Journal of Conflict Resolution 41*(4): 580–602.

Young, Oran R., ed. 1994. *International governance: Protecting the environment in a stateless society.* Ithaca, NY: Cornell University Press.

———. 1999. *The effectiveness of international environmental regimes: Causal connections and behavioral mechanisms.* Cambridge, MA: MIT Press.

Zartman, I. William, ed. 1995. *Elusive peace: Negotiating an end to civil wars.* Washington, DC: The Brookings Institution.

Zartman, I. William, ed. 2007. *Peacemaking in international conflict: Methods and techniques*, 2nd ed. Washington, DC: United States Institute of Peace Press.

Zheng, Yongian, and Guoguang Wu. 2005. Information technology, public sphere, and collective action in China. *Comparative Political Studies* 38(5): 507–536.

Zhu, Xufeng. 2008. Strategy of Chinese policy entrepreneurs in the third sector: Challenges of "Technical infeasibility" *Policy Sciences 41*(4): 315–334.

Ziring, Lawrence, Robert E. Riggs, and Jack C. Plano. 2005. *The United Nations: International organization and world politics, 4th ed*. Belmont, CA: Wadsworth Publishing.

INDEX